I0040414

LEFT BLANK WITH INTENTIO

Reserved for my

Autograph

EXCLUSIVE RECOMMENDATIONS FOR
MONI'SOI HUMES BRAND

"It has been a pleasure and honor to have had the opportunity to experience working with a person who knows that success is gained through hard work. Moni is the type of person that takes pride in what ever she is involved in and she never holds back, but will give 100% effort to make sure that the job is done. Take it from me that if you are not doing business with Moni then you are moving in slow motion."

CHRISTOPHER BIG COTTEN-SHOW DIRECTOR FOR BLAZIN 92.3, MACON, GA

"Moni is a woman who follows her spirit, about her family, and she is driven by her ambition for success. Where some see a dead end, she sees another opportunity."

LEON CARBON-DJ SILK, FOUNDER OF CUT DIS ENTERTAINMENT & PHOTOGRAPHY, RYTHYM LIFE, WARNER ROBINS, GA

"Ms. Humes knows what she wants out of life. She is driven towards her goals. This woman is fearless. She courageously goes after her dreams. Then after obtaining them, she pushes herself even further. Now that is an example of determination."

SHAKIRA BURGE-ORTIZ -OWNER OF WILDER DESIGNS

"Moni has been an inspiration to me and my brand. The lessons given and taught to me by her has created a new vision in my own brand."

SHANDA REAGOR-PUBLIC RELATION ASSISTANT FOR RAGE BELLA RA

"Working with Moni'soi Humes through the years has been an eye opening experience and very productive. Her brand is like no other, very exquisite, tasteful, fashionable, and marketable."

MERVE STEPHENS -CEO OF PSTAR LIVE, LIFESTYLE PROMOTER OF RAGE BELLA RA' & MONI'SOI HUMES BRAND, VEGAS, MIAMI, ATLANTA & MACON, GA #PStarLive

"Moni'soi Humes is a beautiful, diverse, & powerful Queen on the throne of luxury. She lives to be an inspiration to thousands with her styles, ambitions, business attitude, and her loving approach to life. She has never been the type of person to give up on her goals and dreams. She has allowed what God has shown her through vision and meditation to push her forward in faith, just as an eagle she only see's the top of success."

SHADAYAH WALTON -ASPIRING WRITER & ENTREPRENEUR

THE

PR PLAN

OWN YOUR OWN BRAND

The Ultimate Guide to Building Your Own Brand

MONI'SOI HUMES

PR PLAN

Heaven on Earth, Inc {Publishing}

Ordering Information:

Quantity sales. Special discounts are available on quantity purchases by corporations, associations, public relation & advertising agencies, and others. For details, contact the publisher at the address above.

Orders by U.S. trade bookstores and wholesalers. Please contact Heaven on Earth, Inc., Publishing Department: mhumes@live.com

rbragency@gmail.com or visit Author's website www.monisoihumes.com

Booking the Author for speaking engagements, events, and book signings. Email rbragency@gmail.com

Printed in the United States of America

Publisher's Cataloging-in-Publication data
Moni'soi Humes
PR Plan: Own your Own Brand / The ultimate guide to building your own brand/Moni'soi Humes;

ISBN-13: 978-0692403754
ISBN-10: 0692403752

1. The main category of the book —Business —Public Relation 2. Marketing & branding-From industry perspective 3. Leadership

Photography by Leon Carbon

EVERY DAY IS A FASHION SHOW AND THE WORLD IS YOUR RUNWAY

-COCO CHANEL

DEDICATION

This book is dedicated to all of the PR Gods and Goddess of the industry, who understand the value and importance of the process of branding.

I also dedicate this book to the real people who were in my life regardless, even when the fake friends showed their true colors. Real friends over the BS!

Much love and respect to my entire team. I love you dearly for sticking by my side through the good and bad. We are family and it is all love at the end of the day.

"You will not be who you are supposed to be, until you learn to operate on a level of your own self-mastery."

OWN YOUR OWN BRAND

CONTENTS

FOREWORD

By Van R. Johnson, II

When it comes to success, life, and branding it is all a process that Ms. Humes understands. Just as a caterpillar becomes a butterfly, it is a difficult one. This metamorphosis, is traumatizing as there is a complete transformation from what one once was to what it will be. This process sheds the appearance of the past, but retains the experience of the past. The creature that emerges is majestic, beautiful, and colorful with wings that will allow for new ground to be traversed, new places to be visited, and new experiences to be had.

The same can be said for Moni'soi Humes, who has transformed from what she was, to what she is, and will be with a new calling, a new direction, a new spirit, and a new purpose while never forgetting from whence she came. The sum total of these experiences are shared with us in many different mediums, #MoniTip, # MoniWisdom, and #MoniLove

She has a story to tell and we are blessed to be the recipients of these experiences.

PROLOGUE

{moi} is french translated to english is {me}

Somehow long ago in a world that only existed to moi. I developed a flair for living exclusively in the land of fairy tales where the dreams that existed only existed in the mind of my own brand's intelligence. People I met, knew, were friends with, or even in a relationship with would tell me, *"Get out of fairy tale land."* I thought hey, *"What if I made a life out of being the Fairy Tale Princess?"* Hey when I am in fairy tale land dreaming, all I could see was a realm of possibility. In real life thou, I am a full fledge PR goddess who is not afraid to own up to my own brand.

Growing up my mother was such a private woman, I developed this gift for being great, and protecting my own brand from my mother's ways of doing things. God is a genius, because the things you don't understand growing up, he will give it to you in the form of a mom. There you have it, I have been endorsed from my mom who stamped **PRIVATE** on my forehead, and it is more than quite all right with moi.

I merely stumbled across discovering the fashion &
entertainment PR goddess inside of moi. God gave
moi a neat way to showcase it.

Luv you,

THE PR GODDESS

EXCLUSIVE INVITE ONLY

By Invitation Only

Dear Reader,

If you are reading this book, it is because you have an exclusive invitation from moi to "Own your Own Brand". I love my readers; therefore it is my dual obligation to help provoke your brand's intelligence. I grew up with the understanding that it only took a little to create a lot, and the goal is to get it to multiply. This is why mothers all over the world can create a meal from merely nothing. This book has my own special personal touch. I wanted you to feel and know just how special you are to moi while you are reading it.

I am so happy that you are now a part of my Private Guest List.

Ladies and Gentlemen,

Get up, get styled, grab a notebook, The "PR Plan," and head to Starbucks for a cup of coffee. You are in for a real PR treat that is so sweet.

Moni'soi Humes

{Entrepreneurial spirit}

A soul that refuses to quit pushing forward as a boss, a brand, in business, and in many endeavors regardless of what comes their way they continue to build their own wealth.

LUXURY & LIFESTYLE BRAND MISSION

It is the exclusive mission of my brand to awaken & ignite the fire {Kundalini} that is within you, and spark the light of luminosity of your brand to shine as bright as a diamond.

My addictions

Luv, Fashion, & Starbucks-I am a writer

INTRODUCTION

DON'T LISTEN TO ANYONE WHO HAS NOT LEARNED THE KEY TO SURVIVING ON THEIR OWN.

I was 19 years old, just graduated college, just received my Master Cosmetologist license, and there was nothing that you could tell me. Once you know that making your own money is achievable, you are going to keep that mindset. Once you see at an early age that you are capable of easily making $300-$700 in a day as a teen you are stuck with being a leader for the rest of your life.

For me, I was living at home with my parents and I wanted to be grown, but my Mom kept telling what to do. You know we are all like that when we are young. We think that we know everything and no matter who we meet or know they could not possibly understand nothing that we are going through. The mind of a child is the only explanation for this form of thinking.

One day I come home with this child like mindset and my mom and I get into it. I had just about enough of her telling me this and that, so I told her that I was moving out. She responds to me that I was not ready. I respond to her that God is able to do all things. At the age of 19 I was determined, I had lived on my own practically already at a young age, and I just started living with Parents again at the age of 16. Life had thrown so much at me that being strong and surviving on my own was just apart of my DNA from God. I did just that. I did not know how, but God blessed me immediately with a job working in a hair salon cutting hair of all races. I really enjoyed what I did for a living anyway. I really enjoyed working with people of many different races. It was a great experience for me indeed.

I had a huge sense of making it from just my own personal challenges at an early age. I knew the value and the importance of depending on God.

I knew that God plans for me were awesome in every step, strategy, and movement that I made. I have never been afraid of making a decision, even if those decisions did not work in my favor. I lived off the fact that I did not want to wonder things. I knew that I had this uncanny desire to achieve an enormous amount of success with my life at an early age and I had already proven that by graduating at 19 years of age from college. I went for things on my own. Even till this day I see so many people who live in fear and who never live the life that they can live, because they are afraid of the outcome. I could never be like that. You only live once, you might as well go for it while you are here.

Life taught me to be thankful for all my trials, even the screw ups, especially the screw ups, and to not be so hard on myself. Trust me everyone else will take care of that for you. When you begin to accomplish, people will begin to hate on you for a reason only known unto them. Just embrace life and all the events that come along with it, there is a reason God is allowing you to experience all that you are going through.

CHAPTER

1

EVENTS WILL CHANGE YOUR LIFE

Pay Attention

It was the month of February 2010 and my life, my body, and my existence was preparing to experience a sequence of events that would change my life forever. As we stood outside of the parking lot of a club in the state of Georgia, I and my close friend just had the time of our life celebrating her 29th birthday. Now on this particular year, it was leap year so her birthday did not actually fall this February. I remembered it being so weird as weeks prior to celebrating we saw signs, events that continued to show us and warn us of what was about to occur.

As we stood there laughing, knowing that we were not in the position at the moment to drive, we made the decision to allow one of the males that hung out with us for the night to drive. We questioned him, because we had not seen him drinking, however we wanted to make sure. He assured us that he was sober and that we were in good hands. There were a total of 7 of us altogether in the vehicle as we prepared to go out to eat breakfast before we would decide to go back to our vehicle to drive back home. No big deal.

On the interstate, headed towards Riverside Drive in Macon, Georgia, my friend Shannon tapped me on the shoulder as she sat in the back seat directly behind me, *"Girl I love you. This was one of the best nights ever. You really came through as a friend on my birthday,"* she said to me while looking as happy as ever.

My response, *" I am glad that you were able to enjoy yourself, besides my birthday just had come in the month of December and you did the exact same for me. "*

In one moment our life was about to change forever. Just that quick the vehicle swerved as it began to flip I knew that what was taking place was about to change my life forever, *"God I am not ready to die. My family needs me; please do not take my life now. "* These were the only words that I could speak and have time for.

All black was what I saw as the vehicle began to continue to flip over the guard rail. I was told it flipped at least 5 times and hit a telephone pole, however I do not remember. As I lay there in the darkness in my physical body, I hear an inner voice say unto me, *"Get up or you will die here, no one will even see you. "* I knew that it was God's spirit agreeing with what I openly said in power. *"I am not ready to die! "*

I believe till this day that my spirit got out of my physical body before I even had a chance to get off the ground. I literally pulled my will up and told it to, *"Rise."* My immediate thought, reaction, and words were, *"Shannon, where are you? "* I looked, yet I still felt no presence of myself in my own body. I looked into the truck. I still did not see her. I looked on the ground. I saw her wallet and I picked it up. Still no signs of her.

Someone that I knew came on the scene. They saw the vehicle flipped over and I guess they wanted to see if they could help. They looked at me. She said, "*I can't deal with this shit.*" She left the scene. Not too long after that an ambulance had arrived on the scene. I was still looking for my friend. Right when the guy from the ambulance grabbed me, I looked over by the tree and I saw Shannon's body lying on the ground. I attempted to run to her, but the man from the ambulance would not free me. They put me on the ambulance bed, and rolled me into the ambulance. I still felt no presence of my physical body. I remember saying, "*I have to help her.*" The guy in the ambulance said something that I will never forget, "*Be quiet! Your friend is dead!*"

I began to feel tears run down my face. How could this man be so heartless of life? I began to feel the presence of my physical body. Tears began to flood from my eyes. I know even until this day that if my spiritual will power was absent that I would not have had the will to get up. My friend's death woke me up. She literally was sitting behind me in the vehicle that we were in, which meant that her body flew over mine in order for her to land in the front of the tree that was positioned directly in front of the truck. It made no sense to me how this could happen. The only conclusion I could come to was the fact that she was ready to leave this world. I understand this now that life would occur only through a series of events.

It took me months to re-cover from the pain; however the hurt, the anguish was still there. My life was changed forever, everyone I knew I no longer spoke to, no parties, and no drinking. I did not even know how to enjoy myself for a while. The series of events were tragic for me; there were only a few individuals that I kept in contact with outside of my family. I changed my cell number. I could not wrap my finger around what happened, 7 individuals, and she was the only one who lost her life. Although others were injured, it just made no sense to me. To top it off later I was to find out that the driver fled the scene and flew to Paris.

Back at the emergency room:

When I arrived at the emergency room still crying, I fought everyone around me. They had to strap me down literally to keep me from looking for Shannon. I still wanted to know what was going on, everything was so unreal. Laying on the bed in the emergency room I woke up and I heard this voice of a woman as she says, *"I have not seen a woman with her will power. We had to strap her down just to keep her still."*

I still could not understand. I was not wearing a seat belt. I was sitting in the front seat, ejected from the vehicle; my eyes were black, bruised, lips cut, swollen, legs bruised, jaw cut, glass in my back and legs.

The thing about this event was that prior to it taking place. We were planning to leave to New York. Shannon was going to support me as I followed and pursued a career in fashion. While there we were going to shoot our own, exclusive video footage of the entire venture as we would take on the world. This event change my life, how I felt, and what would happen after.

I had survived one of the most tragic events of my life. A year later I began to heal, however I was still in pain. There I was standing in the Boutique of a friends store and she says to me, *"You have to come out of this. You are still alive. Your friend*

wants you to be successful. Now you must want it
too. Stop crying. She sees you, let her see you
happy."

I chose that day to wake and heal. In the year of
2012 I decided to pursue a career in the
entertainment industry, this time as a new woman,
as a fighter, with strength, and as a brand. This is
when I began to push the brand of Humes. I realized
that there are many individuals who are faced with
traumatic events and never move pass them. They
sabotage their own greatness, because they feel
guilty for living, and for having the opportunity to
still pursue their own success. They die in tragedy
and never face life again. They walk around barely
living, and afraid to own up to their own life,
lifestyle, and lively hood. I learned from this that
life was about going against the odds and winning
especially when you are in pain. The pain that you
experience is only a part of the building and the
training process. God is within you and you are the
only one who can activate your brands power.

I had to rise above my own pain to push past all
the events that I was faced to live and build my own
powerhouse.

CHAPTER

2

BRANDING AGAINST THE ODDS

Staying in your lane is so not called for.

What exactly is staying in your lane? When I hear someone tell me to stay in my lane, I automatically hear someone who is afraid. This is how this world is, the industry, and it is filled with individuals that do not want the next person to step in and do it better than them.

On the interstate, traffic is horrible especially if you live in Atlanta, New York, or Los Angeles. LA to this date is by far the worst traffic that I have ever been in. From the Los Angeles airport to Hollywood, over an hour and a half in traffic, you will literally see people on bicycles moving faster than you in a vehicle. When you are heading to a meeting that is important for you to arrive on time, you will want to add an extra 1 hour and 45 minutes to ensure that you arrive to your destination on time. You may also want to change lanes, because it seems as though you are going nowhere really fast at that. The average person will not move, however the individual that goes against the odds is already prepared to figure out how to manipulate the traffic to get to where they are headed. Now it is very dangerous, but one time I remember riding along the side of the interstate to maneuver my way through the traffic. I am not suggesting for you to break the law, but I am suggesting that sometimes you will have to take a risk to get to where you are going.

When I began to step out on my plan I was ready to just do me. I knew that my personality existed in a place of its own. My biggest issues existed with were individuals of my own skin color telling me that I would have a hard time due to the color of my skin and being the face of my own brand. This would follow with, *"It would just be easier to hire a Caucasian woman to be the face."* I have no problem with any woman, but I for sure did not have a problem with myself either. I was ready to look adversity in the face, even if she was the color of my own skin.

I disagreed with them 100%, I knew what I was capable of, even though I was hearing people tell me that I was going to lose. I knew that I had to go against the odds and fight the good fight of faith. I knew that once I made my mind up, it was made up, and there was nothing no one would do about it. It was official. I became and embraced my own brand. I did not care who liked it. I loved me enough to start. I knew that people would fall into the knowledge of my existence as long as I refused to not give up. I embraced to power of knowing, what others believed lost my interest quickly.

Some of those who are against you majority of the time are envious of who you are that they become your competitors. It is so important to know your competitors, because they are usually the ones who want to work with you, follow you, and want to be with you every chance they get with the goal to steal.

7 THINGS YOUR COMPETITORS ARE DOING:

1. Following your every move as they read everything that you post online, yet they never like what you post

2. Watch your You Tube videos with no subscription

3. They are constantly asking you, *"What are you doing?"* all the time

4. Spying on your intelligence

5. Researching on how to do you better

6. They are focusing on out doing you

7. On a mission to bring you down

When I was younger I use to run track from this I knew that your competitors are also helping you to increase. By knowing that you have competitors who are working to out do you, you work harder to stay on top of your game. You turn your focus to your brand to give it a competitive edge.

It is your job to focus on constantly improving your brand. It is your baby. It is your dual obligation to help your brand develop to reaching its full maturity. Don't be afraid to run when everyone else is standing still doing nothing.

It is your choice to either stay on the ground or to take off flying, but you will have to do something different, especially if you are going to go against all odds. You brand deserve the chance to win.

CHAPTER

3

PLAN YOUR BRAND

Every brand needs a plan. When I realized that I was not only a public figure, but a brand I started drawing out my story board literally. My wall, cabinets, and mirrors all had post it notes stuck to them all throughout my home to remind me that I had a story to share with the world. In the year of 2012 I began to model for some fashion shows, from there I began working with a radio station to gain experience in radio and advertising. My experience in promotion went back some years, at least to the year of 2007. I had experience from working promotion for Lounges, hosting open mic nights, and coming up with creative ideas for events as an Event Coordinator. All these things were preparing me to work in the industry as a brand with knowledge and the proper experience to operate in the success of embracing my own brand. I did every position that I worked to the best of my ability until I out grew it.

I eventually recognized that I had a desire to encourage others to operate in their own talent. The more people that I helped; the more I found out that they mis-understood my purpose. My life was heading on a path of darkness fast with no answers. I could not understand the level of rejection that I was receiving all due to the fact that I was standing out more than others. I had to figure out what I did not know; as I began to attend events with the local radio station, live broadcasting, and concerts I found that I loved something about the industry even more. I truly enjoyed life in the entertainment industry. Limo rides, networking, and always being on the go was not what I loved the most, I enjoyed the rush that it gives me. I was learning to appreciate myself as a brand.

I was having the time of my life doing what I love to do, networking, meeting new people, and building industry relationships. I started a bond with one female in particular in whom I was putting on or introducing to other people. I saw something in her; I wanted to encourage her to success. The thing about me is when I see greatness in someone I encourage it as much as I possibly can. That is just me, until I realized certain characteristics that I did not want to be associated with. There are some individuals that you just do not want to be associated with; these individuals are the ones in whom are willing to do whatever to get to the next level in their life even if it goes against all morale.

The thing about life and about business is the fact that you have to have something to offer to people in whom you want to do business with. When you are working with entertainers, celebrities, and high end clientele you cannot put them on a higher pedestal than yourself this will put you in a different category. When you are branding you, the focus is you and your brand. When you get caught up with the wrong people, bad association will get you all the time. People were accusing me of things that I was not doing, just by and from my association. Ladies you must know the females that

you allow into your circle, can play many tricks;
same to you fellas.

What made me truly think is when someone in
whom you know comes to you to say someone said
something bad about you, is "Why they were so
comfortable to say it to you?" I wanted to know
what was being said. It is my brand. People were
saying that I put myself on another level; I was
stuck up, & bossy. I thought hmmm, I can deal with
that. Keep talking, they looked at it like it was
negative, I looked at it like I was building. It does
not matter what they are saying the only thing that
matters is what you are doing and how you respond
to what is being said.

I overlooked all that was going on and all that
was being said after another sequence of events, I
had to go back to the drawing board. I need to plan
Rage Bella Ra. I did not know where to start,
however since I build the energy up from working
with the radio station I got offered to work as a
Manager with my friend as my partner for a local
club in Warner Robins. This was an experience in
itself. This was truly #teamnosleep. I was willing
with the incentives of gas money every day for
work, in addition to a monthly salary. Not too bad!
Right!

The plan was for the venue to have concerts with some celebrity bookings. It was agreed that by me working there that I would be able to give access to Rage Bella Ra.

Rage Bella Ra by the way was the name of the entertainment company that I started. Another incentive to me, during this time we had concerts featuring Young Dro, Rich Kids, Field Mob... this was a lot of work, however more experience for me, until something changed my mind after being in the business for a while. I got short changed on my money. My partner and I got out the game quick and we bounced. I learned real quickly that in this type of business that money had to be paid daily like the gas money. Hell, but I had made a lot of connections. I don't believe in sticking around too long with people who are not willing to keep their word. We got paid; it just was not what we were told.

A few weeks later my Photographer hit me up, he said, "You want to work PR this weekend?"

My response, *"Sure I would love to, but what exactly for?"*

He responded, *"Some NFL's players. Demayrius Thomas and Anthony Allen are coming into town for a party. Let's get out. This is a good way to shake those bad experiences off."*

"Ok, cool let's do it! We need some content for Rage Bella Ra anyway," I said with excitement.

We met up with everyone at the Marriott. We waited out front in the lobby until the limo arrived. I had also invited my friend, who was still dealing with the radio station, but she ditched them to hang with us. Why not right? I still was overlooking the truth. I do my best to see the best in everyone. I use to anyway, now I see things for what they really are. Little too our surprise the radio station was to see us again, this time wondering how I was still moving forward as a brand. The radio station that I was working with had a real issue with me and could not understand it.

No one can stop your will power. When God wants you to experience something that is what it is. We had a great time that night. It was full of energy and great fun. When the night was over the limo driver took us out to breakfast and he spoke with me at the table, *"You know I see and meet many people driving limos and you are just like those celebrities, your personality, your attitude, and the way that you carry yourself. Everyone does not have the ability to shine like that; it is a gift from God. Just be careful of who you keep around you, because they may seem like they are for you, and it could be the furthest thing from their mind."*

I took heed to this. I also knew that I had a long road ahead of me. It seems as quick as I got into the game, I was getting out just as fast. Most importantly God was moving me from glory to glory just like he said.

"Don't get caught up in the people around you, their goal is to use you. God's goal is to move you."

Long story short this friend of mine crossed me in many ways, along with other females that I knew that I helped. It was ok. I could deal as long as I continued to grow. What happened next?

The radio station that I was working with, called me in to tell me that I stood out to much from everyone else. They also said that some people in high places were threatened by me. OK! Cool, not bothered by this, but I took it as a sign that it was time to dis-connect from all these individuals and move on to the next level. I am all about growth, if I outgrew what I was around then so be it.

The association was starting to be bad for my brand. I began to feel as though I fit nowhere; however I shined bright as a diamond everywhere that I went. I did not do this intentionally, it was natural.

I knew that as long as I worked in the industry that I was going to have to make moves on my terms. I knew that I wouldn't have an issue with myself, beyond the fact that I am extremely hard on myself. It was time to focus on my own brand. I had realized that no matter how much I loved people that I am a Boss, fitting in was not my option. I threw the thought of fitting in out of the window, I stood out entirely too much.

It was time to turn up as self, if someone had a problem with it that would just be on them, not me. It was time to put Rage Bella Ra' Entertainment, into full Ra' mode.

Fashion shows

Media coverage

Public Relation

I still saw more, so I decided to bring my own team on board, some worked out, and many didn't. I definitely realized who my solid foundation people were. I also notice the people who couldn't stand with me and who would see me again. Laughing! The same bridge you cross, you may have to cross it again. Don't burn bridges. If people cut you off, let them; however don't let it phase you, and don't you be the one doing the cutting. Just keep pushing forward.

> *"Never look down on anyone, never diss them, because you cannot stop a go-getter."*

Look up at the sky, the stars are few, but if you keep looking you will find the ability to look and appreciate the stars ability to shine especially in the darkness.

The hardest lesson that I had to learn was, *"How could a person who everyone wanted to be around, be lonely?"* I was lonely. I knew this was my choice, in order to live the life I wanted I could not afford risking anymore distractions in my life. I had to spend some time with me. I had to understand more about why I was going through things that I was going through. This also would increase my value and my brands value.

"The quality and state of your brand depends on your level of personal privacy & your value when in public places."

Do not oversaturate the market. Branding can be similar to sex, if you continue to give it away to the wrong person-it will have no value. If you put your brand, your product, and your services in the hands of a person of quality, character, and integrity they will help your brand to prosper and grow, we all know that some people will always work to imitate you of to produce the boot leg version of your brand. On the other hand, there are individuals with the mindset and the desire to save for the real deal.

Let's get smart about it! Create a **Smart Goal** to accomplish your plan!

SMART
Specific, Measurable, Active, Realistic, and Timed
GOALS

This is the perfect way to bring reasoning to your vision. Most individuals have great ideas and / or concepts, yet they still lack the understanding and the logic of the process of following through with a great plan by creating smart goals.

INDIVIDUALS WHO ALL PLANNERS SHOULD STAY CLEAR OF:

1. People who say, *"It is in my head. I don't need to write anything down."*

2. People who say, *"I know what I am doing. I don't need to write anything down."*

3. People who say, *"I remember everything."*

4. *"I was going to, but I hate writing."* (Hire someone.)

5. *"I have not found the time."*

6. *"I am too busy, but I will get around to it."*

7. *"I am waiting on a friend to do it for me."*

8. *"I was going to, but I don't have the right tools."*

9. *"I am not good at writing that type of stuff."*

10. *"I don't see the reason why I should have to."*

Listen! No plan equals = no success. These individuals have a bunch of reasons why they are unable to act on what they see and they have the nerve to be mad at the fact that you won't listen to them, give them your time, or help them. Trust me when I say that these are some of the laziest individuals, don't get me wrong I believe that all wealthy people work hard. I also know they are working hard so that eventually all they have to do is enjoy their time. When you start off lazy and unwilling there is no way to manifest your potential.

You must be willing to work for what you want. The crazy thing is that every successful individual reaches a point where they must come into contact with individuals like this. It may be a friend, relative, or someone that you have hired. The truth is that they are talented individuals who are not just willing to do what it takes. Read more of, *"What it Takes"* from Chapter 5, of Success is what you make it. I make mention of this chapter of my previous book a few times in this book, because I know that it is very prevalent to your success.

The sooner you accept the fact that people who fail to plan should have nothing to do with your vision, the better off you will be.

10 THINGS THAT A PLAN DOES FOR YOUR VISION:

1. Gives you a road map

2. Becomes your guide

3. It is your source for your business

4. It is your way to where you are headed

5. It is your plan of action

6. It is your strategy

7. It is the light when you are in the darkness

8. It is your motivation to remember, "Why?"

9. Keeps your mission in front of you

10. It is how you will get others to follow the vision. No plan! No action!

Plan to take action!

Work the plan until it looks, feels, and sounds like you want it to. It is your name on the line. #MoniBranding101

CHAPTER

4

MY TRIP TO WEST HOLLYWOOD

How I became a water walker?

After working with the radio station, I had built relationships with a few individuals. One in whom use to promote for No Limit and work with David Banner when he first came out in Mississippi. He really inspired me, and pushed me. He told me that he saw me making it and big. I agreed of course. He was speaking on something that I knew for myself, but he was waking up my sleeping giant. He connected me with an artist out in Los Angeles and told me to just go out there, and see for myself how I would like Cali. He said Cali was the perfect location for me. Now it took me a minute, but eventually after long thought and a vision from God I said, *"What would it hurt to walk in faith?"*

After I heard the female artist song, *"Loose Myself,"* by Imani Chyle. I fell in love with her music. She told me to come out to LA to just see if I liked it out there and it would also give me a chance to check out her live performance. She was preparing to do a show in West, Hollywood off of Sunset Blvd at the House of Blues. I was down for it. I was excited. This was my first time in Cali in the year of 2012. I planned to stay there for two weeks. Why not?

I must say that I was really nervous about flying to California. This was a new venture for me; on top of that I was going to meet strangers and stay with them while I was there. These nerves are absolutely natural just make sure that you don't allow them to destroy you and keep you from reaching your destination. Take huge strides in faith when God confirms that it is a go.

The first night of arriving, I was jet lag. When I met Imani, she told me I was a water walker. She said that some people never move in faith.

The show was on that night. I rested for about a good hour and half, and then I showered, and got dressed. Cali was definitely my type of place. What the promoter told me was right on. I loved it.

Headed to the venue down Rodeo Drive, butterflies in my belly, *"I am in Hollywood and the energy here is perfect for me."* We had about another hour before her show was to start and let me tell you she rocked it. She is definitely great at what she does.

There we were on Sunset Boulevard and I felt a certain type of way being there. I felt proud of myself, because I was where I wanted to be in the position that I wanted to stand in. It did not matter who believed in me or not, again I was where I wanted to be. It was perfect for me. I had no desire to see anything else. The Hollywood side of me that was missing was found in California.

I was in love with Hollywood. I connected with individuals there right off the bat. I was where I was supposed to be. There was something else on the inside of me that I had yet to discover. I knew that if I was going to take where God was taking me seriously I needed to get focused on my brand.

There was still more that I needed to know about working in public relation in the industry as well as the corporate world. This was a very exciting time for me and I could not wait to get up the next day just to do it all over again. I knew that taking leaps in faith was the thing that I needed. I was ready to see more, meet more people, and do more.

The next day, the artist took us all around town. Later we decided to venture out even more in LA. I had some people with me, and at the time I was working with a male artist who flew out there during the same time. It was perfect. The right time means a lot when it comes to your branding. Timing was positioning us for achievement.

We went for a ride to see more of California. It is such a beautiful place, outside of all the homeless people that are there and listening to all the stories of individuals that flew to Cali with the same ambition, but did not make it, or ended up living on Skid Row. Living in Los Angeles, California was not a joke. You have to go there with an agenda, a plan, and goals to reach or you won't win there.

Early in the year of 2006

I had a mentor years prior to this day from Queens, NY. He went by the name Cash and he taught me this, Code of Survival: *"Tell No one, I mean no one what you are doing. They will do their best to stop you."*

I spent approximately 6 weeks of just learning from Cash. He had worked with Diddy when he lived in New York when they were younger. He taught me the ugly side of the world. He showed me how shit really was and to not get comfortable with the people around you, because at any moment things could change. Now I was only a seamstress at the time, so I felt like maybe this dude was a little paranoid. The more time that I spent learning the more I found out that he really knew what he was talking about. I was learning from a real hard core street thug, who knew the hustle, and the streets. I was developing the skin for the life that was ahead of me.

One night he decided to take me on a ride with him. We pull up to another vehicle, which was all black, and out stepped some Italians. This is when I learned that it is best to not see shit. I was told that if I did see anything that I was dead. Did not scare me, well maybe a little. This experience was preparing me to deal with all types of individuals without ever being surprised by anything.

God has his reasons for leading me to receive Cash mentorship and besides I don't believe in mistakes, only divine moments that occur and happen in our lives. I learned my fair share of business and I learned that I couldn't survive on my talents, nor my looks. Looks only get you so far, when you go through those doors, you will have to know what the hell you came for. This is the business of The PR Plan. Prepare for the greatest show of your life.

{Back in Cali}

Anyway, Imani, and a group of us went for a ride to Compton. Now you know in my head I was like *"What the hell?"* I really did not want to see Compton. I am a Rodeo Drive kind of woman. She showed me where Tupac use to live. We also went for a drive to Long beach. Hours later we stopped at a gas station that was somewhere in the hood, this would soon be the first argument between the artist and myself. But this was Cali and Imani just wanted to make sure that I got a taste of it all on a real level. Imani is an awesome Queen in all her strides of her own greatness. I truly love and admire her ambition.

I mean go figure, you take two Boss females, and put them in an environment when the two of them had to come to some type of mutual agreement there was bound to be some type of frustration. It did not go like we thought that it would, we got into a huge disagreement. We exchanged words a bit, then we realized that we had nothing but respect for the realness that we both had for our own stubbornness along with our ability to take charge for who we are.

We knew that we were on our real, grown woman shit. It was nothing but respect from the two of this from this point on.

After a long day we decided to have a glass of wine, a few people came over to chill, and we had dinner. The next day I was ready to get back to work. I was beyond excited. Imani spent some time just telling about the industry, the parties, and the many realms of possibilities to explore.

The next day a few of us drove out to the other side of Los Angeles, heading towards West Hollywood. We visited the Dash Boutique. It was a nice store, a little different from on TV. No paparazzi outside! I think that with the Kardashian's ladies not being there would explain a lot.

As we walked up Melrose, there was so much I wanted to see and stores I wanted to go in, Louis Vuitton, Burberry, Coach, and the list went on. The energy and the vibes that was connecting with had me on cloud 9.

The next goal of course while we are near the Hollywood Hills area was to head straight over for the Hollywood sign. Besides I wanted pics of me standing in front of the sign. It was hard actually getting that close, so I just turned around with the sign in the background, and then boom. Say cheese! We call this photobombing.

Once we were done taking pics, I called the male artist who came out to Cali as well to meet us at the studios in West Hollywood. Imani had hooked me up with a producer while I was out there, so I booked some time for the artist to record while we were in town. We ended up having a blast for the rest of the night. The engineer was an awesome person with great energy, and good vibes.

Our night eventually ended at the studio. I think that it was around 2 am so we headed back to the house in Los Angeles. We had a few meetings while we were there and I discovered that true water walking is to do it scared and know that God has you every step of the way. It will turn out better than even you expected.

Remain open to learning of others and expanding your territory. I knew this would not be my last time in California and it has not been. I have been there several times since then, because it became apart of my PR Plan to market my own brand in Cali.

CHAPTER

5

BUILD A PRIVATE BRAND

Real leaders lead in quiet. They have an enormous amount of respect for their own privacy and they conduct business with individuals who have the same respect for their own privacy. It is important to maintain extremely high levels of confidentiality. Below I have listed careers and fields who value privacy.

1. Private bankers

2. Financial firms

3. Public Relation Agencies

4. Managers

5. Lawyers

6. Publicists

7. Psychiatrist

8. Counselors

9. Mentors

10. Private corporations

11. Survey companies

12. Hospitals

Then of course you have those who are constantly releasing information into the public. These career fields are required to make public notice of all of their decisions, meetings, minutes, and budgets.

1. Government

2. Politicians-Democrats and Republicans

3. Newspapers

4. Media

5. Non-profit organizations

6. Salons-a place that most people go just to gossip

Most people who know me personally know how private that I am. I am so private that I remind those who are real close to me often to pick and choose who they bring around me. If I don't know them, I don't trust them. It may seem like a little bit of being paranoid, however trust me that if you want to be successful at what you do you must be picky about who you have around you. The funny things is that I know and deal with all types of people, industry people, corporate individuals, entrepreneurs, politicians, hustlers, bosses, church goers, moors, mason, and some of your everyday people. I am just wise in my dealings, because I know that in all that we do that if we lack wisdom then destruction is soon to be found. Make sure that you build your team with people who have the same value, and know your circle well. You don't have to keep it small, just know it. I for one am not a huge advocate for circles. I understand it though. It is apart of the process. Your goal is to get your team on a straight path. If your team is going in circles there is no progress begin made.

You need a big team to do big business, to enter larger territory, and to expand with the blessings that God gives you.

People are resources, those who say they don't deal with people will also lack in resources. **No resources equates to no success.** The more you understand what you are doing, how you want it to be done, and how private you need to be about it, success will just flow.

Years ago in the year of 2011, a friend of mine called me up and asked me if I would ride with them somewhere. I said sure of course, I knew that the only time that they would really call me was if they needed a friend to talk to. Weird enough I needed someone to talk to myself, I felt like I was at a confusing place in my life.

They picked me up and once we took that drive, they wanted to go grab a bite to eat. As we sat down at the table, we began talking. They began to tell me that there are 3 circles, the poor of course, the middle class, and the rich, while they were talking they were drawing an illustration on a piece of paper. Well, when people make it out of the poor circle and move to the rich, because no one cares about the middle class, they live comfortable. When people make it out of this circle at the bottom, if they were to look back, the rest of the rich will kick them out of the circle that is just the way it is. I am telling you this he continued to say so that you know that you don't need to worry about what you are losing, just keep going forward. Then he did the weirdest thing as he looked at his food. He told the lady at the register of the fast food restaurant, *"This is not what I ordered. I don't eat onions. I know that I said this to you at least 3 times when I placed an order."* The lady got an attitude with him and he responded, *"If you don't like your job then quit, because you are in the business to take orders. Don't be mad at me, because of your own decisions."* Then he grabbed me and said, *"Lets walk around this place."* We did that as well. The morale of the story is the free and the rich do what they want to do and the poor do what they are told to do. Pick which one you want. Live with that decision.

This touched my spirit it made me feel some type of way. It was what I needed to know for the reason known only to the universe and now to you.

This conversation on this day put me in a different zone to just embrace me, because the rich are getting richer and the poor are getting poorer. The rich are also private.

This is why I say that you should consider becoming private about your business. There are so many individuals who are capable of so much success and they set themselves back with drama, telling their business to the entire public. It should be our main goal and mission to strive for success in all that we do, yet we make it so hard to live a life of greatness just by getting in our own way. It is time to trust and know that there is something in you that will light up once your ignite that internal fire.

Keep your eyes on God, because he does not want you to look back. He reveals his secrets to those who are able to hold them. When those secrets are opened unto you by invite, treasure them, and just go forward.

CHAPTER

6

BRAND DIVERSIFICATION

{Brand}

It is what identifies you from the rest in your marketplace.

Every individual that is an entrepreneur at some point in his or her professional career will create their own products and services to offer to consumers to buy. When they reach the level of promotion and marketing, those products and/or services they will begin to ask their selves, *"What makes me different from the rest of those who are out there and offering similar products or services?"* This is a very great question and one that you must answer. If you don't answer the question, consumers will find a way to work your business for you. Instead of them following you, you will begin to follow the consumers. When the consumers change, what you offer changes. This is not what you want for your business, what you truly want is to "diversify your brand." You want to focus on creating a brand that can weather the storm, according to Entrepreneur.com

It should be your mission for your brand's value to be high. This means that no matter what trends come and go, consumers know to buy into your brand. They know that there is so much value in what your brand offers that they want to be affiliated with it. This is why affiliate marketing and network marketing has become so huge in today's society. It gives opportunity to all regardless of their race, nationality, background, and education. It is sad, however there are so many companies who have pre-judged individuals off of these very things. We all know that it is illegal to discriminate against anyone, yet in still we know it plays a major role in who gets hired, promoted, and who receives an increase. That is just the way that it is and these network marketing companies saw a need to help all

If you are not in network marketing you are missing out on the possibility to put a small effort into a huge success.

people make money. If you are not in network marketing you are missing out on the possibility to put a small effort into a huge success. Every successful person who is successful has done some form of network marketing at some point in their career.

Network marketing is a vehicle to help individuals brand their own business, whether it is for them to increase in speaking skills, increasing in their leadership, elevate in their level of management, or getting trained on sales and marketing; the door is wide open through the vehicle of network marketing to brand your own business, services, or to market yourself as I am to increase in speaking and increase in publicity, and book sales. It is an avenue that all heavy hitters take even those who are in illegal professions take the route to operate in network marketing. Dope boys understand the jargon of purchasing wholesale, markup, and a private network. This is why when you can show them a legal way to operate, some of them will take it. They are just switching products and brands.

People buy from brands who are not only consistent, but brands who are able to relate to them in some form of emotion while providing them with the value that they desire.

According to Forbes.com the "World's Most Valuable Brands"

1. Apple brand's value $124.2 billion, revenue $170.9 billion

2. Microsoft brand's value $63.0 billion, revenue $86.7 billion

3. Google brand's value $56.6 billion, revenue $51.4 billion

4. Coca-Cola brand's value $56.1 billion, revenue $23.8 billion

5. IBM brand's value $47.9 billion, revenue $99.8 billion

6. Mc Donald's brand value $39.1 billion, revenue $89.1 billion

7. General Electric brand's value $37.1 billion, revenue $89.1 billion

8. Samsung brand's value $35 billion, revenue $209.6 billion

9. Toyota brand's value $31.3 billion, revenue $182.2 billion

10. Louis Vuitton brand's value $29.9 billion, revenue $8.7 billion

11. BMW brand's value $28.8 billion, revenue $81.3 billion

12. Cisco brand's value $28 billion, revenue $47.1 billion

13. Intel brand's value $28 billion, revenue $52.7 billion

14. Disney brand's value $27.4 billion, revenue $23.6 billion

15. Oracle brand's value $25.8 billion, revenue $38.3 billion

16. AT&T brand's value $24.9 billion, revenue $128.8 billion

17. Mercedes-Benz brand's value $23.8 billion, revenue $98 billion

18. Facebook brand's value $23.7 billion, revenue $7.8 billion

19. Walmart brand's value $23.3 billion, revenue $304.4 billion

20. Honda brand's value $23.2 billion, revenue $115.5 billion

If you look at the top 20 of this list, you will notice that Facebook is the only Social Media Platform that is on this list due to Facebook's ability to understand the power and importance of branding and connecting its audience through human emotions. As you scroll through your timeline and you see your old class mate who just gave birth to their first child, or you read that someone just started their own business, or you read about a new product launch. You are given the opportunity to connect with the masses just through understanding that there is a world of pain, happiness, success, opportunity, and individuals from all across the globe that you are able to connect to online.

Facebook also provides the opportunity to start your own campaign and advertisement around your brand and for a specific target audience whether young or old it is there for you to create more revenue. Facebook also allows you to start a fan page that is free of charge, yet you can include a link to your own store, Instagram, Twitter, Pinterest, or even an Etsy store. Take advantage of these opportunities and unite your brand with its target market. Make this your priority.

Your goal should be to provide consumers with your brand by expanding what you have to offer. You should give your customers options. The last thing that you want to do is limit yourself to just one product or one service. Facebook is constantly growing; every time you turn around their company is doing something new, and they're getting those who use Facebook to market their brand. Facebook users are also Facebook marketers. When you log online to post about your brand, you are not just promoting you, you are promoting them without them paying you. They figured out a way to get its users to work for them for free. Consumers are spending countless hours on Facebook. We all know that time is money. We save them money, while they make $23.8 Billion in sales a year with a market capital of $159.67 Billion a year.

Mark Zuckenburg, the CEO of Facebook won, because he created a strategy and he executed it until it worked. When he faced adversity, he dealt with it through creating effective solutions. He built a brand that would function in helping individuals find their classmates, old friends, and meet new people in different demographics.

When you are working to establish yourself, you want to also look at your products, its functionality, your geographic location, and it's packaging. You want to start creating a strategic plan on how you will move forward in your own brand, and your own uniqueness.

When it comes to "branding" I really learned through hands on hands experience, school, internships, and through having mentors. "*Most individuals experience repeat failure, because they fail to learn their own craft.*" Your craft is your personal DNA, your makeup, and it is who you are.

When you are establishing a name or a brand for yourself you must also create a list of benefits that your brand will offer to your consumers. Once you do this, you will need the permission of consumers to market to them. You will only have one shot to convince your potential client(s) that you have the best product for them and if you build your brand correctly they won't need convincing.

"Without a selfish reason to continue dating, your potential customer [and your new potential date] will refuse you a second chance if you don't provide a benefit to the consumer paying attention, your offer will suffer the same fate as every other ad campaign that vying for their attention. It will be ignored."

-Permission Marketing by Author Seth Godin

Consumers are like your partner in your relationship they want you to care about them. If you cannot connect with them in anyway, they lose interest, trust, and loyalty in your product(s), services(s), which is your brands identity.

Your brand has to say something to the people. It is your obligation to discover your message and deliver that message to your target market. Your message is your story and that is what people will be able to identify your brand with.

There is no individual that walks the

face of this earth that has not been through a storm. Everyone has a story that another human being can relate to that will help them understand the value of your brand.

It is so important to remember that we are not just in business; we are people who must engage with people in our daily lifestyle.

Start online engagement through the posting of online content

Brands that are surviving online are engaging consumers with online content. Google Analytics has the capability for you to log into your Gmail accounts, add your link for free, and obtain a tracking code to track how your online website and content is engaging your target market. This is important, because your target audience is your potential fan base, consumers, and buyers.

The more you put into your brand, blogs, social media pages, the bigger your return will potentially be. You are investing your time into your success. This causes for strategic action. Story boards are a great way to help layout your content. The purpose of a story board is to find your way through the tunnel. It is your visual map to your success. You have to visualize it first, because without a map, you are "blind posting."

What does it mean to blind post?

-blind posting-

Posting with no agenda

Trust me we all have done so at some point, because either we don't know or we have no one leading us in that department, or we are being led by blind individuals. There is an old saying stating that the blind cannot lead the blind, therefore your brands message has to shed light to the masses of your own target market.

CHAPTER

7

KNOW YOUR BRAND

We were taught that the only way to prosper in anything is to believe in it, and that is great as it is a step in the stage. The next level after believing in what you do is knowing that what you do will in fact work. When you reach a level of knowing it prepares you for the hard times that are ahead of you. It is the only way that you are going to survive when hard times come your brands way.

Believe-: a state or habit of mind in which trust or confidence is placed in some person or thing

: Something believed; *especially*: a tenet or body of tenets held by a group

: Conviction of the truth of some statement or the reality of some being or phenomenon especially when based on examination of evidence

Know-: to perceive directly: have direct cognition of, to have understanding of <importance of *knowing* oneself> : to recognize the nature of : **discern**

: to recognize as being the same as something previously known : to be acquainted or familiar with, to have experience of

: to be aware of the truth or factuality of : be convinced or certain of
: to have a practical understanding of <*knows* how to write>

archaic: to have sexual intercourse with
: to have knowledge
: to be or become cognizant —sometimes used interjectionally with *you* especially as a filler in informal speech

    When people face hard times and adversity, you will rarely hear them say that they are about to revert back to what they believe in, people revert back to what they know. This is why it is so hard for people to transform into the greatness life has to offer them, because someone told them that their belief system was off. Well, they are not living off of what they believe in anyway they are living off of what they know.

Once you know that what you are doing can be done, you will live differently, you will act differently, and you will think differently. There are several factors that are going to attack you.

Your brand is a person in itself, which means the same issues that you can face are the same issues that your brand will face.

EXAMPLES OF THINGS THAT YOUR BRAND MAY FACE:

1. Who is the face of the brand?
2. What is the nationality of that face?
3. Are they black or white?
4. How much do they know?
5. Are they old enough?
6. Do they have enough experience?
7. Culture & Religion attacks

All brands are attacked by discrimination.

You will reach a point when age attacks, color attacks you, your race, your nationality, your religion, your culture, and your social & political status. This is all stemmed from what you know and what you don't know. This is all history and knowledge that you must dig deep into and truly know thyself. Do not get caught up in the stage of building your faith, know that your faith will work indefinitely.

What you receive in this life is all about what you know, who you know, and how you put forth the action once you know. If you don't get to this phase you will quit when you face any battle that seems so hard.

Believing in anything has to be built into having faith. There are levels to life, to learning, to living, and to knowing. You must know that what you are about to do is going to take time, do not hire people to join the team or your company who are not willing and patient enough to put the time and effort into the projects that you are working on. **Branding is based and built on infinite time, so do not put time restraints on your brand's success.**

Some of these top marketing organizations tell you that one of the most important things is having a belief in what you are doing when starting and building your organization and yes I agree, however it is when you surpass that vision that knowing the way becomes more important. Your faith will get shook up, but when you know that you know, there is nothing that will stop you from pushing forward. This is why some individuals quit and some keep going. It is the fact that some know that what they are doing is going to work and some don't.

Great knowledge is like great leadership it will continue to push and coach you to the next level. Once you know something you must give an account for what you know. This is because once you know something it will never leave you, it becomes apart of who you are. It is embedded in your DNA.

I could never for the life of me understand a person who knows who they are and say they chose not to be who they are anymore. The only explanation that I could come up with is that they have not acquired the correct knowledge of who they are as of yet. They have been living their life off of lies instead of the truth of the correct knowledge.

Gaining access to the correct knowledge of who you are is what you will need when it is time for your brand to survive.

CHAPTER

8

HOW TO SURVIVE ON YOUR OWN BRAND?

You may not always discuss how to survive on your brand; however ultimately you want to know how you can survive on your own brand? Oprah once said she didn't feel successful until she didn't have to work to worry about paying her next light bill.

> *"You won't make it, until you can survive on your own."*
>
> Eric Thomas

Eric Thomas said, *"You won't make it, until you can survive on your own."* This is what our focus is to know how to work our business, visualize your vision, & a profit off the value of your brand or cash out. It is kind of an oxymoron, but your brand cannot survive until you stop caring about what others think about it.

Branding is about making your own mark, telling your own story, and sharing your brand with a specific target market.

There are so many artist, designers, and creative individuals who have forgotten the importance of branding. Branding is a part of your marketing. It is how consumers recognize you from the rest. It is a mark that is so distinctive that it identifies who you are and what you do. Your brand tells the world who you are.

12 THINGS THAT HELP OTHERS IDENTIFY WITH YOUR BRAND:

1. Color(s)

2. Mark-logo

3. Name

4. Company

5. Website

6. Product

7. Services

8. Marketing material

9. Presentation

10. Sales and delivery

11. Your story

12. Location

During the A3C Festival I had the pleasure of attending a panel discussion on the subject of "Branding" with fashion, music, and your company. It was a pleasure hearing Ms. Skittles speak about www.cupcakemafia.com, which is a fashion company that she started with a couple hundred dollars. She graduated college with a degree in "Fashion Merchandising." She spoke about the most important part of her company is maintaining her brands identity.

This is so important, because it has a lot to do with how consistent you are willing to be in the market place. In the world of fashion, you have to be ahead of the game. All fashion industry people are at least one full year in advance, magazine run times are 6 to 12 months in advance. You are entering into an international market that will require you also to know culture, this is also important to your brands survival.

The wrong words, gestures, behavior, or an accidental insult can cause you to lose the biggest or even the smallest deal or client of your life. You want to be able to relate to all people, all the cultures that you enter in to do business with make sure that your research how to properly conduct business with them first. Business laws change from state-to-state. Don't learn this the hard way like I did.

Business owners, brands, companies, and moguls must do the work and the research. Those who want to survive will stay up late nights looking for the next big idea, the latest trends, and new pantone colors that hit the market. They also look at red carpet styles.

Your image is how you look, put together your wardrobe, how you wear your hair, how you can look like no one else, and how you walk fierce every time you walk into the room.

There is a distinct difference between you and the rest. You are a superstar. Remember that if you are not willing to go all in, someone else will come along with a better idea, and work harder to take your position. Don't ever get comfortable, your enemies seek to destroy you and when you least expect it they will attack.

Don't work to recreate the will, work to create a system that works for your brand according to the will that is already written. There is no point of changing something that is not broke, change what is. God has written a will that is so unique that it identifies us in our own category and he set it on a solid foundation.

A foundation that others can come on and flow freely. You have something special that others desire. All you have to do is operate in it.

When you are working to survive, you will stay in a zone, because you know that if you don't that your brand will die out.

If you really want to see your brand succeed, continue to feed it. Stay hungry!

Life is for Living not Living up tight

Jay-Z

"Younger will get younger every year!"-Forever Young

CHAPTER

9

PROVOKING YOUR BRAND'S INTELLIGENCE

Laughing who does not want to live young forever, it is possible but only if you build your brand correctly.

What is in you must come out, if not you will live your life carrying information, stories, books, ideas, concepts, clothing lines, music, and content that will go to waste. All you have to do is find the value in whom you are. No offense, but people physically were made to take a dump daily, "Why?" Our physical body is unable to hold the food that we put into our body, so it turns into waste, and it passes through.

What was once there is now gone, therefore what you once had access to will no longer be available, this is how our intelligence works. I have met so many smart people filled with intelligence, yet I have questioned their intelligence, because they do absolutely nothing with it. They don't turn their intelligence into great teachings, books, product(s), businesses, brands, property, or seminars. They never utilize their own intelligence and it goes to waste, because they only share it with their friends who they often are smarter than anyway. Robert Kiyosaki is a firm believer of, *"Keep it simple stupid."* The friends who have no where near as much intelligence as you reach for the stars with your great ideas. Learn to have no value in your own brilliance. Stop giving your greatness away to individuals who did not earn it.

Being and owning your own brilliance is about bringing and adding value to your own brand. I transcend all of my gifts, talents, abilities, and creativity into increasing in my own writing. It is how I operate in my own intelligence. It is my way of sharing information with the world. I know and I acknowledge that my physical body can only hold so much information, therefore I release it when it is there in the form of a new company, a new business partner, or a new product.

"You lose what you don't appreciate, value, or operate in"

Some individuals are down right now, yet the only thing they need to do is to lift up someone else. That is how our intelligence works, it operates under universal laws. What you give is what you receive.

If individuals knew how intelligent you were, they would seek to destroy it. This is not true. If others knew that you were so intelligent, they would buy into your brand, hire you as a Creative Director, or ask you to oversee their companies marketing. They understand that there is just as much value in hiring an intelligent being to truly market their brand(s), product(s), or service(s) for the right publicity. They may even ask you to be CEO, President, VP of Marketing, or invest into your brand.

Do not fear releasing your intelligence. It is far more dangerous to walk around carrying all that power, because one day it will explode out like a ticking time bomb then it will be too late.

Know your worth. In the song "Young Forever" to me the song is about branding. This song is about accomplishments, the life that we are supposed to live, as you listen, you will begin to feel that if you would repeat the words that you can as well live that same life of living. The question is, "Do you really want to live forever?" Consumers want a brand that can provide an experience for them. Period! Either you provide it to them or they move on to the next best thing. That is just how branding works. At the same time they get what they pay for, if they have a small budget, they will get small efforts. If they have a big budget, they will get large efforts. When taking on PR clients, it was just a part of me to give as much as I possibly could to the client. I had to learn that if you are not careful in the giving that people will take advantage of the giver. Lay out your plan, put it on the table, and charge what you are worth. If you know that they are not paying you anywhere near your worth and that you will not even put the effort into their project then your best bet is to turn it down right away. It is better to just stand your ground. If you need more experience, then work the position that you desire increase in it to the best of your ability that way the next time you can increase your price. Know your value as well.

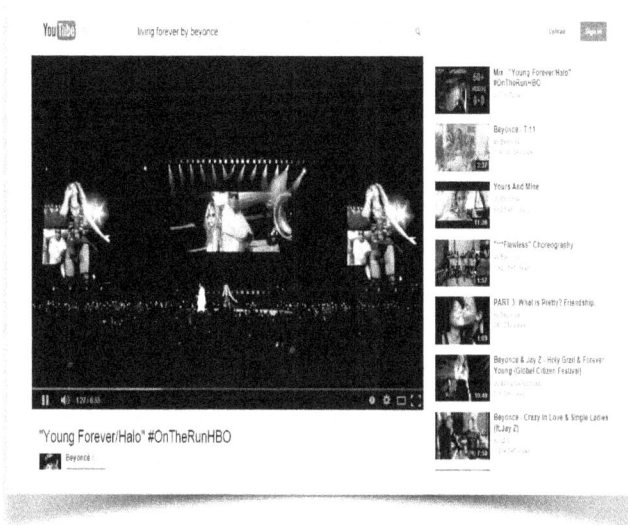

"Young Forever/Halo" #OnTheRunHBO

BECOME A POWER COUPLE

Shawn "Jay Z'" Carter's net worth is $560 million

Beyoncé's net worth is $450 million

Together they earn over a $1 Billion together- this is a power couple. As a couple the two were named the highest earners in the entertainment industry by Forbes.

What make this couple so awesome is that they are so powerful alone. Jay-Z steps in the picture and he does something that most men, average men, even powerful men would not dream of doing. He is fearless of embracing his woman's power. The fact that they are able to demonstrate two distinct brands that are able to unify them as one brand. The fact that they are able to do this, *"Provokes their brands*

intelligence." Consumers want it. They buy it.
Beyonce and Jay-Z look the part, dress the part, and
they handle their business. They are partners on top
of that, while still maintaining to their own
individual brand goals, consumers want this, bad!

They have brand value, it has opened the doors
for them to create something that is untouchable,
and something that is able to live forever.

God put a physical shell on your spiritual being
to show you what he could do. He wanted us to see
one another, then he gave us the power to create the
unseen. That which is unseen will never see death.
It is incapable of death; it only correlates the
language of life.

Knowledge is so illuminating that some people
are afraid of its secrets. Knowing is a part of your
value, your message, your intelligence, and your
brand. You cannot reach your full potential unless it
learns to know itself. You must learn to be knowing
of who you are. Once you understand and know
your worth, you will begin to build on that alone.

According to Entrepreneur Magazine article;
"Entrepreneurs should pay close attention to how
Beyoncé has built her brand. Beyoncé's concert tour
of the Mrs. Carter show sold $1.8 million tickets in
over 126 international dates that generated $212
million in revenue. She has not only built a brand,
she has connected with consumers, her fans through
her songs that empower women; Single Ladies, Put

a Ring on It, and Run the World (Girls). She is definitely fierce in her strides, but it is the name, the brand that she has built that has generated the revenue. She has a message and she is constantly delivering that message to her fans, giving them a sense of empowerment. Much respect is given to her Publicist who has protected her household name with her dear life. What you hear about Beyonce is what Beyonce wants to be heard.

This world exists with some incredible individuals who have reached a level of understanding that true success of anything is built through partnerships. Once you reach the level of working as one, you will make and produce so many streams of income that people will want to join your projects, volunteer, intern, partner, sponsor, and assist you and your brand in its intelligence.

Individuals already know that it takes intelligence to understand the power of partnerships.

CHAPTER

10

WHAT IS GOING ON IN THE DIGITAL WORLD OF MARKETING?

According to e-Marketer between the years of 2013-2017 the number of digital video viewers in the US is expected to increase by more than 22 million. Individuals, brands, and companies are finding You Tubers who match their target demographic are teaming up with them to market their products and services.

89% of customers are influenced by online reviews and reputation

91% a mobile phone users have their phone with them during dinner and while their out on the streets 24-7.

9% of average revenue increases with one additional listing on Yelp

Consumers are spending more time on their cell phones, tablets, and their laptops, and computers. Their mobile devices are more convenient for them to access Instagram, Twitter, WordPress [I make most of my blog post, directly from my cell phone], Facebook, Tumblr, LinkedIn, plus many more apps.

A LIST OF WAYS TO REACH THE DIGITAL WORLD OF CONSUMERS:

1. Websites
2. Phone apps
3. QR Codes
4. Digital business cards
5. Email marketing
6. Mobile websites
7. Social Media platform(s)
8. Search Engines
9. Digital newsletters
10. Digital distribution
11. E-book downloads

12. Music digital downloads

13. YouTube

There are so many sites out there to buy followers and likes, but your goal should be to gain organic followers. What are organic followers? These are individuals who follow you just because they love your brand.

This is your audience and you need to make sure they are real people, if you want to turn your post into revenue. If your followers are robots then this will be hard to do. This does take time, you may only have 100 followers, yet those 100 followers you may only be 10% of those who buy from you. John D. Rockefeller said that, *"I would rather have 1% of 100 individuals efforts than 100% of my own."* Rockefeller was the Founder of Standard Oil Company. His knowledge of success was something that he earned through hard work and ambition to do more than the average person was willing to do.

This is what you want to look at when it comes to social media. You are working and building from the inside, not the outside when it comes to your revenue. Looking good is only part of the battle, you have to turn the time that you invest online into clients, team members, and revenue, or it all will become pointless. Do you want to waste time? It is up to you, yet remember that the rich buy time.

You have to take the time to engage with these individuals who are liking your post, following you, or purchasing your products. You need this to keep your business growing.

Make sure that you check out my Instagram profile by the way @monisoihumes and Follow moi

CHAPTER

11

OUT WORK THE POSITION

Passion is an awesome gift to have, but we all know that passion can also stir up some things within you. Let's stop for a second and pin point what we think about when we think about passion.

There are so many energetic words attached to our passion that with too much passion it may cause you to overwork, overlook, and deny yourself of building the greatest brand ever. This is why when employers are looking to hire individuals they are looking for individuals who possess the qualities of the position.

When I began working in the field of public relation I knew that I developed a desire to increase in the knowledge of PR in the fashion, music, corporate, and entertainment side of the industry. Most importantly I wanted to know PR for the purpose of my own brand. I also knew that I learned better through hands on hands experience. I was offered the opportunity to work in public relation for Atlanta International Fashion Week. The truth is that my passion was so strong, that I was willing from day one to out work the position. The position as a public relation manager was big, so I had to get in there and get my hands dirty. I had to do more, the more than I did, the more that I learned. The challenge was more exciting than I knew. The passion that I developed for the position involved me through the entire 12 months of the internship. I knew first hand that public relation and marketing was no joke. What I realized more than anything was that my passion is what it took of me to build my own brand, a lifelong, and lasting image. I saw interns who made it. I saw interns who couldn't handle it. I also saw individuals who fail to finish, because they were looking at the money.

"When you are hungry for success, you cannot look at the money. The money will take you from being hungry to losing opportunity."

When an individual is hungry they work with focus, dedication, and a strong will to accomplish. They understand that as long as they keep going, the money is already theirs. A person who focuses on the money is also focused on the things that will distract them.

9 THINGS UN-SUCCESSFUL INDIVIDUALS KEEP THEIR FOCUS ON:

1. They focus on their current situation
2. They focus on what is going wrong in their personal life
3. They focus on their past
4. They focus on how hurt they are
5. They focus on how much pain they are in
6. They focus on their heart ache
7. Sickness constantly knocks on their door
8. Death rises up frequently in fear
9. Un-belief sits in their heart
10. They focus on all the things that have not worked and that they feel will not work

These individuals only see now and that is ok, just understand that they only play a temporary role in your story. They are an extra. They get paid to walk through. They want what they can get right now and they are not willing to learn beyond that. It is all seasonal.

Then there are those other individuals who have taken the fact that they understand that hunger and thirst occurs simultaneously. You see what you do naturally is only metaphor of success. When you reach this level of branding, it is all about building through and to phases.

Everything grows through different levels of the pyramid. As a brand you must learn to adapt to change until you are transformed into your true brand. This is how consumers will identify you from the rest. Your name plays an important role into your success. There are some individuals that do not reach any level, because they destroy the value of their own name before thy even come into a self-realization of who they are.

Individuals who say, "*I am worth more than an internship.*" You have not learned the process. Individuals who say, *"I am not doing anything for free."* It is a part of the process. All great brands are great due to the time that they served to the process of becoming great. They placed value in the knowledge that they received through the process. They did not look at it like they were interning, they looked at it like they were gaining valuable information.

A list of individuals & companies who knew of the power of internships, branding, & good old fashion hustling:

1. Myself
2. Karl Lagerfeld
3. P. Diddy

4. Russell Simmons
5. CoCo Chanel
6. Valentino
7. Louis Vuitton
8. Moet & Hennessy
9. H&M
10. Government Agencies

All of these companies, brands, and individuals understand the power of knowing the process to get to the next level.

CHAPTER

12

BUILDING YOUR BRAND'S VALUE

"It only takes a little hunger+thirst to build a lot"

How far do you want to go with your brand is the question? This will determine how much you put into its value. When you take the ingredients of hunger + thirst and combine the two the results will be impeccable. Remember the thirsty individual wants to deal with their now situation. The hungry individual(s) desire is to receive the proper knowledge to prosper in all that is in front of them. The combination will manifest what you see if you combine the desire to prosper in your future and your desire to survive now.

Individuals fail to see the process of an internship through; they miss the future ingredients by only thinking that a portion of the information is enough. They don't find this out until they hit an uh oh in a project that needs the information. You will not see these things coming if you are not properly trained for the position that you are working.

The best part of your brand is the knowing of self, the increasing of self, and being fully aware of how to operate in self.

I started the "Couture'A'list de luxe" in the year of 2014. It is a fashion blog that I created to push the brand to eventually launch my own fashion magazine publication. Every fashion, fine art, luxury, and runway news that I post promotes the plan. www.couturealistdeluxe.com

I love fashion and I love to write, what better way to work than to work at what you love. When you do what you love doing it does not feel like work-period. Some days I forget that I am working.

COUTURE 'A' LIST
DE' LUXE

The goal in all that I do is to build the value of whatever it is that I am creating or launching. The Couture'a'list de luxe is a brand that I created to target to consumers who love high end fashion luxury. These are the readers that I attract, the followers that I gain, and the re-post that I get. I watch to see what post gets re-posted. There is certain information that your readers are looking for, some they look over, and some they engage in. The post that the consumers are engaging in you want to document that in your PR notes.

This is how it works, when you take care of your brand, your brand will take care of you. That is how it works fellas when you are in a relationship. What you do for her, she will turn around and do the female version of it for you. Have you ever heard the saying, "Do what you did in the beginning and you will keep her?" Relationships work this way and so does your brand. When you first start investing in your brands value, vision, and mission it is wonderful, because it is all in your favor. When the tough times come do not stop investing in your brand. When you stop going out of your way you will potentially be at risk for taking a lost. No one likes taking a lost, no one.

WHEN YOU ARE BUILDING YOU WANT TO LOOK AT A FEW THINGS BEFORE YOU START:

1. The foundation
2. The structure
3. The ingredients (tools)
4. The glue to hold it all together
5. The crew or the staff
6. The cost
7. The 3 year financial projections

These are all essentials to building your brands value, without the essentials there is no brand.

CHAPTER

13

PUBLICIZE YOUR BRAND

Every artist has a story to tell, that story is what will help them to reach their target market. The problem is that there are not enough artists telling their story, although no one even knows who they are. You have not even established the importance of getting 'publicity'. What you do is what failures do; you build a team just to say that you have one. Team work makes the dream work, unless you are still in a sleeping state of mind.

You hired a manager, promoter, street team, and when they come tell you what they have experienced and how they can help make your brand better you just give them a deaf ear. Remember your manager works for you, if you don't trust their leadership then why did you hire them? The worse mistake you can make is to think that there is no value in others times, but your own. It is time to consider the entire team. Visualize the entire team building as one.

In order to publicize who you are you must first work on the infrastructure. If you don't take the time to turn your craft into a business you are just wasting your time. You must think, eat, live, and breathe the success of your brand. Take a nail, then hammer it in the belief system of BS, it does not work. You have to put the hours into what you are doing to see the results that you desire to achieve for your brand.

BRANDING DOES ALL OF THE FOLLOWING:

1. Connect the story team

2. Creates customer thought

3. The art of corporate story telling

The entire point of publicity is to spread your brand into your target market in a certain way. This is important to the success of your brand. When I first started learning public relation, I stayed online researching. I made it my goal to always be different regardless of how others would respond to it, as long as I would get a response. You may make a post online that receives no likes, yet this does not mean that you did not get a response.

I knew that some of my followers were like me, they were private. There were times that I received no likes online, but I received direct messages online, text messages, or emails. All that mattered was the response.

It can be frustrating when it seems as though no one is paying attention, but you have to be paying attention to them. When you pay attention to them you will begin to notice them watching. Put yourself out of the way, it is too easy to get in your own feelings. The goal is to reach the people, which will take more than your post.

1. Facebook advertising

2. Sponsored ads

3. Banner ads on other website

4. Radio interviews

5. Press releases with PR media distribution

6. You Tube commercials and advertising

7. Google ads-clicks

8. Bloggers

9. Affiliate links

These all contribute to your publicity plan. You must have a budget to spend money towards your PR plan. There are people who absolutely care about what you have to say, they want to know how they can get to where you are or accomplish their own vision. How much will it cost you? You may not have the finances at that very moment, but know when you do receive it-you will already know where to distribute your funds.

When you move forward, it is not just for you it is also for your followers. While focusing on your publicity you want to get the people to listen to your message. The message is what they will relate to. It does not matter if the message is good or bad they just want to be able to relate to it.

Consumers don't like individuals that have not been through any struggle to get to success. The reason being is that no one relates to perfection. All individuals have been through something, this goes back to people relate to people. Perfect people will always bore people, because it is unrealistic.

When you share your story it is all about timing, if it is the right time it will change your life. As great as Beyoncé is, individuals could not relate to her for the longest because they felt that she was too perfect. When Jay-Z became her manager that began to change, she began to show the world another side to her that people could relate to.

Publicity is not about money it is about the people relating to your story and your message. #monibranding101

The way you deliver your message can change at any point in your career; this is up to you, and the direction that you want your brand to go in.

I kind of made my life hard for myself by knowing publicity so well that I became way too private. Others wanted to know more, this is why I decided to write the "PR Plan," so I could begin to share my story with the world. This is only part of it, but from here on I will continue to share the dark side of my life, along with the light side of my life.

There were many days that I felt that no one cared, and that no one believed in me; this made me feel like I just wanted to quit. Those days will come and go in the life of all entrepreneurs and without those days you would not have the ability to look at another entrepreneur and say that it will be ok. You have to go through the battle first before you can tell someone else that it will be all right.

When you are ready to launch your brand, map out the dates, your news feed, your timeline, and how much money you want to invest into your PR Plan. If you don't want to do it yourself, email my company rbragency@gmail.com

You don't have to do it all yourself, put a team around you that is willing to put just as much time and effort into putting your brand out there. People like to be affiliated with people who are affiliated with other people.

People want to know that you are not just talking about yourself, but that other people are also talking about you. Don't try to clean up every mess that is made, let your publicist orchestrate what needs to be said directly to the media for you.

It looks better when the media says, his or her Publicist said today. Some things don't deserve your response. Let the people talk. Let the people wonder. Let them talk to one another about you, because as long as they are talking they are publicizing you. It is better they do it than you. No one likes the fact that you are confident about you, but they love the fact that others are confident about your brand.

Don't overdo anything, but in all brand efforts use moderation.

1. Don't allow too much bad news to be out in the media
2. Don't allow too much good news to be out in the media
3. Live in balance.

As we conclude this chapter, just remember all brands need publicity. Just focus on creating a great PR Plan, having moderation, and trust in your brand even when the people are talking about you. Let them advertise you and promote you to the next level.

CHAPTER

14

MARKET YOUR BRAND

Of course you have a desire to bring your family,
friends, and loved ones into the fold of what you are
about to introduce to the world. It is lucrative to
you, well so you think that it is any way. As a brand
we all desire the support of these individuals that
are close to us; however we also confuse them for
our target market when they aren't. Your brand will
reach the masses when you learn who the masses
are for your brand. It is hard to be tenacious about
branding yourself when you are still in the

discovery stages of learning who your target audience and market is, where they are, what they look like, and what they drive.

When you do discover your market, allow them to see you develop, change, and transform as your brand goes through those developing stages. People are prone to follow individuals, brands, public figures, and companies who are growing. If they have been following you for 4 to 5 years and you have not launched a website, product, blog, or business you may need to just fall into the *#FriendZone* and leave the *#BrandZone* for those who are putting in the time to market their brand. It is crucial to the success of your brand to understand what needs to take place.

I personally have experienced the failure of mixing the two; it is hard to make this work, because family, friends, or loved ones sometimes will not respect the value of branding yourself. You want to separate them from your professional life. There are only a select few that will respect what you do and who will also be loyal to what you have to offer to consumers.

Let us start be making a list of questions to answer to build your own target market list.

21 QUESTIONS THAT WILL CHANGE YOUR BRANDS LIFE

1. What are the age ranges of the market that you desire to reach?

2. Location-Where do they live? Market segmentation{Neighborhood, geographic location, zip code, so forth}Nielsen & www.census.gov Research, because population surges are happening in the physical and digital world.

3. Who are they? Males, females, or children

4. What do you want them to get from your brand?

5. What is their income level?

6. Where do they work?

7. What do they drive?

8. What brand(s) do they currently wear?

9. What type of product and service do they enjoy?

10. What are their hobbies?

11. What do they do for fun? Hobbies, etc…

12. Are they single?

13. Do they have a family?

14. Do they live with their parents?

15. Do they live in a luxury apartment community or do they own a house?

16. Are they smokers? Drinkers?

17. What is their favorite color{s}?

18. Are they apart of any other organization?

19. What is their level of education? High school, GED, college, or College graduate.

20. Are they currently enrolled in school?

21. Are they an employee, self-employed, or a business owner?

This is called collecting or gathering information. The best way to start this is to answer the questions for yourself first. I will explain different ways to gathering data later in this chapter. Your brand identity is your brand and it is built based on your own personality. If no one likes you, it is because you are displaying unlikeable characteristics. You must also learn to develop your own personality. I have met many individuals who are crafty, talented, but they lack a developed personality.

"If you want friends then show yourself to be friendly."-Dale Carnegie and God

Whatever you desire you must first become the thing in which you desire. By becoming what you desire you are manifesting what you are offering first, those who give more than others usually are those in whom desire to receive more in those same areas. These are universal laws of releasing and receiving, whatever you put out into the universe you are also asking for it to return back unto you.

It was a weird time in my life and I asked God to shift me to a different environment, around different individuals, and the spirit moved in three days. I was able to work with very prominent individuals in the field of marketing. As I dove deeper I understood that the 5 P's in marketing would have to play a major role, below I have listed each one, and the role that they all play individually to the marketing of your brand.

1. Product-What you have to offer to your consumers.

2. Price-How much will it cost? This also determines the quality, whether it is a luxury item or not.

3. Place-Where do you want to market your product to?

4. People-Who you're going to market your products(s) to?

5. Promotion-advertising, promotion, sales channels, distribution

When we start out in business we fail to understand that branding has to do with publicity. I remember sitting down to the table with a client that desired me to do all of their marketing for them, yet they did not realize all the levels that there were to marketing. There are so many different umbrellas under the roof of marketing.

- Public relation
- Advertising
- Branding

- Communications
- Community involvement
- Direct marketing
- Global marketing
- Media planning
- Social media marketing
- Pricing
- Product Design
- Selling-promotion
- Supply Chain management
- Marketing plan
- Distribution
- Integrated marketing communication (IMC)

IMC-*Are ways to gather the consumer's intelligence and how you communicate with the consumers.*

Seller's market-demand *outweighs supply*

Buyer's market-Supply *outweighs demand*

Do not be afraid to plug your brand into your market. Your brand will be as great as you understand the market place and how well you market what you have to offer. Just do not neglect to market what you have.

"Stay on course with your success, own up to owning your own brand."—

When you truly market your brand, you will not feel comfortable; however this will help you reach your target goals on getting your brand out to the consumers.

CHAPTER

15

LOOK, LEARN, AND LISTEN

Conduct research to collect data from your potential clients. There are many ways to conduct research; you just want to make sure that you are obtaining the right information from reliable sources. This is why you must collect first hand primary data through interviews, focus groups, and surveys. You want to know what the consumers think, feel, and suggest.

You also want to collect secondary date from textbooks, Government census, Associations, Internet [Not Wikipedia, anyone can log on here to upload information]. It is the first thing to pop up, therefore don't get tempted they have just branded their company really good. Be willing to work for information, put the time in to gain access. Do not be anxious for anything, but to meet a deadline.

One of my mentors taught me the importance of this technique-to look, learn, and listen. She said if I would do this I would be successful at whatever I put my hands to. Sometimes we fail to pay attention to what others or saying this leads to failure in relationships, friendships, and partnerships.

Author Jay Lie wrote the "Art of Listening," is suggesting several additional reasons to listen to customers:

1. To develop and deepen connection with customers

2. To find new growth opportunities that are right under your nose

3. To increase customer awareness of your products and services

4. To reawaken otherwise dormant customers

Lipe list of ways to listen to your customers through different connections:

a. One on ones interviews

b. Surveys

c. Networking

d. Blogs

e. Customer clubs

f. Referral programs

g. Mystery shopping

h. Basic visibility testing

These techniques are also marketing tools being repeated. Create valuable interactions with your customers about your services and products, as you focus on building your brand, focus on the STP. *Segmenting your potential clients, targeting these segments, and preparing to position your products and services into the marketplace.* You want to become effective in marketing your own brand. You want to understand and learn the personalities, attitudes, and the behavior of the consumers, and your potential clients.

I personally learned business through life, my education, relationships, and love. I saw through a relationship that I experienced with a man that a man can learn you so well that they can use it to increase you. Or vise a versa, they can use it to decrease you, and the same goes with women.

> **STARBUCK'S MISSION**
>
> *To inspire and nurture the human spirit — one person, one cup and one neighborhood at a time*

This is how information works, you use the information to add value to your clients.

You are working towards the goal of constantly gaining information to satisfy a need that your client has, not to turn them away. By helping them to build what they desire, you are also helping to build your own vision. So many individuals fail, because they think about satisfying self instead of satisfying their customer.

When you help others dreams come true, you are also helping your own dreams to come true. This is all based upon your attitude, your delivery, and your confidence. What type of attitude does your brand have?

-This is your brands voice.

What type of attitude does your client have?

-This is your client's voice.

1. Cognitive (What your client knows?)

2. Affective (How your client feels?)

3. Behavioral (What your client does about it?)

When I go shopping I look to purchase items that make me feel a bigger sense of self or to just enjoy the experience of that particular store, shop, or salon. Luxury items are purchased by certain individuals. Just like the lyrics in a song goes, "I am feeling myself, feeling myself,"-Beyoncé This song is giving off a certain vibe, a certain energy to the woman who are listening suggesting that sometimes you should just be into who you are, what you have going on, and be confident about it. Music gives off high and low levels of energy to whomever listening unless you are aware of what is going on. I chose to listen to music that will make me feel a certain way at that point in time of when I need it. I may need to feel that high vibe from a song in particular. You just have to know what you need and when you need it.

People want to feel who they are, when you can service them with a product or an item to help them do so, and they buy into it. I go to Starbucks for the experience, the vibe, the energy, and yes the coffee. Starbucks is a brand, who has become a huge brand and it is showing it through the revenue that it produces annually. Below is a chart of their recent 3 years, starting 2013-2015 from Nasdaq.

Fiscal Quarter	2015 (Fiscal Year)	2014 (Fiscal Year)	2013 (Fiscal Year)
December			
Revenue	$4,803(m)	$4,239(m)	$3,793(m)
EPS	1.3 (12/28/2014)	0.71 (12/29/2013)	0.57 (12/30/2012)
Dividends	0.32	0.26	0.21
March			
Revenue		$3,873(m)	$3,549(m)
EPS		0.55 (3/30/2014)	0.51 (3/31/2013)
Dividends		0.26	0.21
June			
Revenue		$4,153(m)	$3,735(m)
EPS		0.68 (6/29/2014)	0.55 (6/30/2013)
Dividends		0.26	0.21
September (FYE)			
Revenue		$4,180(m)	$3,788(m)
EPS		0.77 (9/28/2014)	-1.62 (9/29/2013)
Dividends		0.32	0.26
Totals			
Revenue	$4,803(m)	$16,447(m)	$14,866(m)
EPS	1.3	2.71	0.01
Dividends	0.32	1.1	0.89

Starbucks Corporation Revenue & Earnings Per Share (EPS)

⊕ Follow

$92.03* 0.45 ⬆ 0.49%

*Delayed - data as of Feb. 17, 2015 - Find a broker to begin trading SBUX now

What a coincidence that whenever you see
Starbucks, you also see their logo with a follow
button. Just click it! They are just brilliant when it
comes to branding. Kudos to Howard Schultz who
made a brilliant career move to move from the
position of Director of Retail Operations to actually
purchasing from the original owners, who
understood as he studied the company of Starbucks,
he also knew the brand.

We should all follow in Schultz footsteps of
brilliance even if we are working for a company
outside of our own brand. Elevation can take place
anywhere, anytime, and with anyone. Be open to
your success going beyond the level that you are on.
Own it, because many consumers identify
themselves with the products that they buy, such as
Starbucks.

Consumers buy not only products that show
forth just who they are; they also buy who they
want to become. #MoniBranding101

I studied at the Academy of Art University; one
of my courses was, Consumer Motivation. I loved
this course in particular, because it taught me the
knowledge of why consumers do what they do. We
all are motivated about our purchases, where we
spend our time, who we spend our time with, where
we shop, eat, and the types of brands that we want
to own. Our motivation is sparked from different
places, maybe emotions, a current situation, an
event that we must attend, or even a luxury buy. We

want what we want and only we know why we want it. I love shopping, because I love fashion and I love to look as great as I feel on the inside.

In conclusion of this chapter, make sure that you look, learn, and listen to the people in your life, and those in whom you are doing business with, it will change their life as well as your own.

CHAPTER

16

YOUR HUSTLE HAS TO BECOME YOUR BRANDS LIFESTYLE

Hustler – a go-getter that is determined to see their brand succeed and make profit.

"Stop looking for Social Media to do your dirty work" – Moi

When you are in a season of planting, getting dirty is a part of the process. This means it is time to get your hands dirty. As easy as you wish the road would be, know that is just a part of life and now is the time to put forth time, hours, days, weeks, months, and effort. Entrepreneurs must do some face to face building in order to get the results that they desire. Put your social media on auto pilot, get out of the house, and attend some networking events, seminars, and network at some parties.

When individuals are not willing to hit the streets and put their brand in the face of their target market, it will not survive. Brands who are winning are the ones who are going against the grain. If you think that you will win without getting out to the marketplace, your brand will not produce any income. Do not let where you are in life stop you from producing. When your brand is constantly producing then that means you have reached a level of being in high demand of the consumers.

I wrote this book based on my own real life experiences. I had people putting me on in my field all off the strength of my ability to know that I was going to make it anyway. Confidence cannot be denied. When you are confident about what you are doing, the product that you are marketing, and your brand, individuals become confident as well about spending their money on it.

Your hustle has to possess the quality of confidence.

10 THINGS CONFIDENCE DOES FOR YOUR BRAND

It is so important that we remember that God told us to never cast out our confidence. God foresaw that our life would have trying times; he knew that we would be fought tooth and nail by our enemies, competitors, family members, and friends to keep us from going forward, therefore he left us a message. Paraphrasing, but the message is that no matter what you face in this life, nor the next do not allow it to cause you to stop being confident in knowing that you are beyond great and so is your brand.

Here are ways to keep your message strong and in the mind of those who follow you.

1. Send out engaging emails
2. Build a list of leads
3. Network, network, network
4. Build relationships
5. Grind for what you want
6. Possess that state of hunger
7. Know that if people walk away it in itself will still pro-create

8. It duplicates itself

9. Does not give up

10. Activates passion daily from a burning fire from within

12 THINGS THAT YOUR CONFIDENCE DOES WHEN YOU MULTIPLY (X) IT BY YOUR HUSTLE FOR YOUR BRAND:

Your goal is to one duplicate yourself, duplicate your system, and multiply your brand. We may start small, however our ultimate goal is to find and hire individuals who think, act, and know just as we do, to build a team of individuals that hustle because they understand what it is like to not have anything, so they grind non-stop.

My goals were one thing, but playing it smart was another. I hate to sweat, if I can create something through hard work to potentially work less, while working smart while achieving the results that I desire then that is what I am going to do. I hate for things to pile up on me, since I know this, it is important that I complete all task on my list in advance for the ultimate pleasure and results.

The goal of branding your products:

1. To make money

2. Circulates out in the universe & returns blessings back unto you

3. Increases your investments

4. Upgrade your lifestyle

5. Builds your legacy

6. Builds enough for your children's children (Inheritance)

7. Multiplies the seed in itself

8. Teaches others of their ability to make it

9. Changes lives generationally

10. It weathers any storm

11. It finishes all races that it decides to run

12. Its mission is not the trophy, but to produce more of the quality of itself.

20 THINGS THAT YOUR HUSTLE NEEDS TO HAVE AND PRODUCE

You are not doing what you do for the fun of it, to those who don't understand your hustle please keep it moving pass them. You are in business to make money, because it takes money to produce the quality materials that you need for your business to be successful.

1. Business cards-digital or hard copy

2. Bio

3. Products on hand

4. Flyers {In back pack or briefcase}

5. People-Brands do not survive without people

6. Media kits

7. Backing Power

8. Website

9. Phone apps

10. Social media, online engagement

11. Newsletters

12. Other services

13. Photo shoots

14. You tube videos

15. Seminars & Conferences

16. Shows, events

17. Exhibits

18. Tours

19. Street Team, promoters

20. Fan base

Once you understand and respect the power of your own hustle, you wake up, and get to it at ease. You will produce in so many ways that many will wonder how, when, where, and why? A hustler is hard to stop, because their grind has and will remain a way of life.

A friend of mine told me when I became an entrepreneur that, *"You have to either get a job or get a hustle. If you don't do one or the other, you won't survive. It is too hard out here. You are going to have to get up and literally do what every one else is not doing times ten. It is way easier to just get a job, you are pretty. I know you are not trying to stress like that, however if you really want to do this-it can be done."*

They laid out for me the positive and negative side of what I was about to face. It can be done. I did it. I am stronger now that I have ever been. It was hard, some months I made more than others. Some weeks were better than others, but my life was 10 times better than others. Why? Because I chose to live a life of freedom. When you chose freedom it opens up so many doors for you to experience so much more than the average mindset. I chose to move forward scared. You must move in the greater you while being completely afraid of it.

CHAPTER

17

THE GAME OF RESPECT

Being a female in a pre-dominantly male industry made it hard for me to prosper; especially being attractive you will encounter individuals hitting on you often. This added more pain to the journey; it became irritating, and frustrating. I had to fight harder, and work harder. I was not complaining about it, however working in promotion, marketing, & branding in the industry meant that I had to fight for my respect. Men will try you and when you resist they feel either rejected or intimidated by you.

Some will even go the extent to lie on you, but know yourself through this.

It would be so awesome if you could start a business and gain immediate respect. Now don't let me leave the women out of this, I have seen females who take advantage of their position as well, if the man does not do what she wants then she moves pass his talent to the next one. This is very sad that it is like this, but it is so real in the world that we live in. The saddest thing I have seen from some of the richest people money wise, is the lack of patience to build their own personal life. This is weird, because the understanding to build is obviously present.

The truth is that when you sit down with your counterpart, it is often that the opposite sex will become attracted to the power that you have, but you have to be stern in your mind for business. Forget having any level of emotion when it comes to these situations. Be reminded to, "Keep it moving forward."

You will notice that when men do business with men, respect is automatic. Vice versa women doing business with women, respect is automatic. You just show a level of respect to the same sex that has put in the same amount of work that you have put in, however most times that level of respect is not shown automatically to your counterpart. It has to be earned, they must know your motive and your agenda.

I learned to develop thick skin, to not feel emotional about certain things when it comes to my business and my brand. I could not allow myself to be thrown off course. I had to grow into the development of a sense of ownership, especially after working for many years just helping others to get established. I knew that I had to change the game. The only way for me to do that was to be in control of my own destiny. Instead of working for companies I would come in as an Independent Contractor under my own business name, this would give the space and the room that would add respect to the resume.

I learned what leaders knew, what millionaires and billionaires knew. If a challenge presented itself, I would sit to the table and overcome it {Brainstorm session}.

If something were to come my way I had to figure out what to do, as a leader that has to become your responsibility. Talent was nowhere near enough for me to be taken seriously; I had to put something behind my name. Talent is only a small percentage of your success. I grew in knowledge, products, experiences, and services. My value had to continue to increase. I was not waiting to be put in a bracket; my goal was to create a way for myself.

I remember one night in the year of 2014, in Atlanta in particular I had attended this networking party with a client of mine at Franski's. I met a lot of individuals and business owners at the venue, and I had the pleasure of meeting Mr. Frankski himself. Well, to the point is later on that night as my client and I were on the interstate, she began talking. She was an older woman who had been in the game of business and managing money for a minute. She said to me as we were conversing, *"Don't you see what is going on? All this shit is just a game and all you have to do is know how to play it. If not they will play you instead. You must stay smarter to stay in the game without being stopped."*

Now I was thinking that she was very intoxicated, however I knew that she was spitting the truth as it is. I knew that at some point in everyone's career everyone had to learn this or it would be a very valuable lesson of being played.

Now she must have not have heard herself, because one of the contractors that she hired defeated her at her own game and with her permission he was given access to the company account, while we were out of town he took $50,000 out of the company account, in addition to purchasing many items on the company card. She was furious, and then she realized that she gave him access. When she realized what happened she was furious, so she stopped everything including her own business. What she did wrong that I learned from, she stopped her entire vision off of one man's lack of loyalty. She put his mistakes and she allowed her entire company to suffer from it. Now she was still serious when it came to her business, she just allowed her emotions to be in play. It happens to the best of us all at some point. Some people play alone, others play with a team, and some just don't know how to play so they sit on the sidelines.

It is a great thing that all checking and saving accounts are covered by insurance, up to $250,000 in FDIC. Since there was insurance covering these the money would be recovered anyway.

There was definitely something going on with the guy who took the funds, but hey who knows? I was extremely disappointed for multiple reasons, the main one is the fact that I am and will continue to stand the grounds of having integrity in business. I have learned that means something different to everyone. This guy had no integrity when it come to business. We had contracts on the table that were worth more than what he stole. Some people are just idiots.

Learn and become knowledgeable about money. The FDIC does not cover stocks, bonds, mutual funds life insurance policies, annuities, and securities. These are all financial products that are owned by you.

Life is about playing as a team, but when you realize that one member lacks loyalty and integrity, instead of getting rid of the team, you get rid of the one bad member. God wanted me to see this, because he wanted me to know what to do and what not to do. When you have a huge vision, never let any one stop you from pursuing it even if you lose on occasion.

When you are playing a game of chest, it is all about the next move. Who is going to make it? Where will it be? How will you defeat your opponent?

In the real world, if they are not on your team they are against you. There are also those individuals who are against you, but do not want to show it until they learn the game from you. When I was naive I had individuals who were against me but they did not show me.

"Don't underestimate anyone's loyalty. It should be proven, tried, and tested; male and female."

It they hate your test, they lack loyalty. In order to respect the game, you must be a great player.

1. Listen at all times

2. Look, pay attention to everything around you

3. Learn from those who play it well.

4. Make your next move, your best move

5. Be prepared to defeat your competition

6. Stay reminded at all times that you are playing to win and so are your competitors

7. Know who your competitors are, don't be naive and say that you don't have any. If you have no competitors, not only are you not in business, but you are not running a race.

8. Look the part for the game that you are playing [You will never see the Atlanta Falcons wearing the Saints football jersey, vice versa].

9. Know it does not matter if they like you as long as they want to maintain a valid relationship with you. Some of your best workers will not be able to stand your success, but let them continue to work.

Relationships are an important part of your brand. The best way to maintain any relationship is through respecting it. You don't have to like what the other person is doing or how they do it, all you have to do is learn to respect the game that they are playing.

CHAPTER

18

MASTER THE LIFESTYLE

In my mid 20's I was introduced to a lifestyle-nice clothing, shoes, accessories, vehicles, luxury apartment, luxury vacations, and limousine rides, and the luxury of sipping on Starbucks at the same time. During this time I was able to watch, look, listen, and learn from multi-millionaires who were players in the game to live the lifestyle of their choice. Although I was not there yet, the fact that I was living the lifestyle, I was becoming a slave to living in luxury. What does this mean? Some individuals are trained to be enslaved to bondage; my desire was to be enslaved to freedom. We duplicate how we allow ourselves to be treated, what we see, and what we hear. The lifestyle was becoming my master, however I had to learn how to master my lifestyle or it would control me. This meant that I needed to take my level of ownership higher. I had to put my priorities into perspective. I had to determine what was important to me and what wasn't.

Now, when you come in contact with this lifestyle over and over again it is because you are supposed to be living a lifestyle of luxury. God does not tempt us. I had to create a name for myself, if I was going to be taken seriously, and then I had to constantly be willing to take enormous leaps and steps in faith.

You see I knew so many wealthy people, but the goal was not to only understand true wealth it was to understand the importance of standing on my own brand just as one would their own two feet. Your name has to be great enough for you. When people desire to do business with you they are not only going to look up to who you are, they will look most importantly to see what you have behind your name.

In order to get what I wanted out of my brand I had to do the following:

1. Maximize my time

2. Increase my own chances of success

3. Develop a strategic plan

4. Open myself up to a higher level of creative awareness

Once you open yourself to the creative energies you will receive guidance to your abundance, your lifestyle, your prosperity, and your own wealth. Most important I learned that these most valuable assets were not found in the material things that I had, but in the products that I created and owned.

This is called inventory!

Liabilities are the things that you have in your possession, but you still owe money for. Why because you don't value the importance of ownership. It is so easy to fall into the trap of debt and working for things that lose their value on a daily basis. By the time you leave the lot with your car the value has de-appreciated. We all know this, so the goal is to one day come to the lot and pay cash for your cars. By the time that you have worn your shoes at least a few times, they have lost their value. You can purchase an item in the store, return it, and the price value could have decrease tremendously just because the store made a markdown. These things don't produce any revenue for you. I am not saying that there is anything wrong with having these things, just remember the goal is to own.

My grandmother once said, *"I don't want any of my family members renting apartments, because it makes no sense to pay on something month after month with no intent of ownership."* She said a mouthful that I for one never will forgot, this was too important. It carries great value.

People pay on all types of things, but let them miss a payment, the lender will remind them of what they have no ownership of. We don't research, nor think deep into things. How can you purchase a new Cannon camera on credit, pay on it month after month, stop paying, still own the camera, but owe money? A lot of things dealing in terms of ownership is done in the terms of 30 days. This is the amount of time you have to pay up, own up, claim, and pay out.

These are all things that we must learn, study, and know, because it is a part of our education. Well, known money educators (Kiyosaki and Donald Trump) teach us the difference in debt, liabilities, assets, credit, money, saving, and filing bankrupt.

Everyone should take some time to spend at the Federal Reserve Bank to study the history of money. Financial education has a lot to do with your brand. Cash has no value, people all over the world are opting to be paid in gold. The only power cash has is the power the people give it.

They are insured and so are you. This is why wealthy individuals spread out their wealth with different financial institutions and other financial instruments. This is why depositors will only deposit $250,000 per account, to protect and keep what they have. The FDIC does not cover your money beyond this amount.

"True wealthy individuals work for ownership, they create a lifestyle that will help other individuals live while mastering their own craft".

Poor individuals work to buy more liabilities with no intentions of ownership. They have no desire to help others, because they cannot see past their own situations. Marketers know this, which is why they place many gas stations and liquor stores in poor areas. Marketers know that poor individuals throw away money, because they are caught up in what they see so much that they just drown in their own misery.

What I was doing when the universe, God, the creator was specifically putting me around a great lifestyle I was not just learning; I was becoming the lifestyle of my own brand.

"Instead of just learning how others do things, we bring our own style and individuality into play."- *Robert* Greene-Author of Mastery

"Instead of just learning how others do things, we bring our own style and individuality into play."

Robert Greene-Author of Mastery

Master your Lifestyle

Robert goes further in his book to speak on the process of leading being the ultimate form of power.

1. Apprenticeships {Learn basics}

2. Creative active {See inside}

3. Mastery {Full clarity}

When you are learning to master your brand you must understand that the plan does not always go as you originally had written, however master the achievement of the flow.

My problem: The universe literally was moving on the behalf of my momentary needs and I was getting caught up in the emotions that were throwing me off course when instead I should have been moving with the flow of the presence and ignoring the ignorance of things that did not exist.

In learning to master your lifestyle, it is pertinent to your brand that you are aware of all factors that must be considered even in your success.

1. Time management

2. Emotional stability

3. Consistent message

4. Consistent appearance

5. Privacy-brands that maintain a substantial amount of privacy keep control of their brands message

6. Studying who you are, your brand, what is new, the market place, and the behavior of your consumers

There are several ways for you to live the lifestyle. There are so many different companies that are on the market, such as Uber. Founders Travis Kalanick and Garrett Camp started Uber in the year of 2009, in San Francisco, California. The company is now branded and available in over 53 countries. What makes Uber so remarkable is the power of it's branding, the way that they infiltrated the market place, and its ease of access. As you download the app, enter a credit card, and wherever you are you are able to get picked up in style.

On top of that you are able to log online, sign up as a driver or as a partner. Sign up and enter my promo code for a discount or your ride. https://www.uber.com/ Enter code: monisoi

On top of Uber, you are able to hire a publicist and gain access and exposure to your own lifestyle. Working in public relation myself showed me the power of gaining the right publicity. It takes work, contacts, resources, power, pull, time, and consistency. Most brands do not have the time to do this or do not understand the importance of doing so, yet when done correctly it will make your brand notable, but also you will be noticed by those in whom matter.

Kim and Kanye are everywhere, now we are not so sure of how they truly got together or if their publicist just thought it would be a really great idea. Who knows, their publicist does.

"Your image is vital to your brands career"

I literally do not like to deal with individuals who do not want to dress the part. It is one thing to not know how to dress, and another to continue therein in laziness and a lack of care for your own appearance. It makes no sense at all to not put forth the effort to look great, feel great, and to put yourself in the position to promote your brand. Social media is there for you to do just that, to stand on a platform that once was not there. Now individuals all over the world at one click of a button can change their entire life.

Pressure comes to see what you are made of. Are you a diamond or are you a fake?

CHAPTER

19

SHINE BRIGHT LIKE A DIAMOND

Stand on your own Platform

Everyone feels the need to tell you to do this, to do that, however I wrote this book to share my brand story with you to tell you to do what works for you. My first book was an immediate success for me. It is a book of poetry, under the pseudonym of ! Myster?ous M!, titled "Who Knew the Fight?" I caught so much hell in my personal life that it literally destroyed me. I made a decision to keep the confusion down to stop publicizing myself. It was causing too much attention to me good and bad. I was not ready for, it, so I backed off from my own success story. This is the moment in your career when you decide whether or not you want to be famous or wealthy? Whatever it is that you are supposed to be, trust me you will know it.

YOUR BRAND HAS TO WEATHER THE STORM

I was younger, so it was a huge experience for me to get all this attention just from writing a book. I learned that your brand has to be able to weather the storm. It just has to take whatever is thrown at it. I had no idea what a brand was as far as I thought into it. Although my product was sharing my own personal story with my readers, I was not in tune with growing into the maturity stages of my brand. The process just slowed down completely, because I didn't want it anymore. I was not ready. You must be prepared when you release a product or service to flow with all the hype before it dies down.

I allowed what I was going through to determine the expiration date of my brand. I let the hype die. I was not ready for the attention, the storm, the rain, and all I wanted was for the sun to shine. Cloudy days-I was not prepared for the things that would hit my life. I wanted the diamond without the process of becoming a diamond. It does not operate like this. You have to prep your brand for it's shining moments and take the bad moments that come along with it, this is known as the process.

The process...

1. Carbon dioxide 100 is buried 100 miles into the earth

2. It is heated @ 2,200 degrees Fahrenheit

3. It can handle the pressure of 725,000 lbs. per square inch

4. When it is finished and formed, it rushes to the earth and cools to form a diamond

This is how your brands survive and are able to stand on its own platform. No one throws away diamonds, once they are discovered. This is why film producers, directors, labels, public relation companies, reality shows are looking to discover the next best thing. It is because they understand the process and they want to become a part of discovering the value.

Then of course you have those that see the value, but they are not willing to put in the work. They know what you are doing. They know it is working, but they are just along for the ride. People have ego's in fact we all do, some individuals are better at managing their ego's than others. When you look at you and then look at your brand, "What do you see?"

Individual → Brand

Visualize them as entirely two separate entities, "Why?" Your brand is your ego, with its own identity, traits, color(s), personality, and when it goes out into the world it is representation of you.

Your brand is the part of you that will never see death. If you promote it, publicize it, and share it with the right audience, market, and consumers; It will be successful.

It seemed as though when I made a decision to embrace being a brand, public figure that it was the most difficult thing to get the support that I needed to help push the process along the way and I had to find inspiration. I had to put myself in the stories that others had already been through and made it out of. Gabrielle (CoCo) Chanel will remain a huge inspiration of mine. She had nothing to start with however she was surrounded by a lifestyle that pushed her to look within herself to pull what was in her to come out. The amazing thing about her story was living with a man who could not see her purpose; therefore he could not help her embrace it. This amazing woman who was soon to become a fashion icon and legacy was being overlooked. She was in the home with a man in whom she still gave value to, because he gave her the experience of living a rich lifestyle to a certain extent.

One day this man introduced another man into Chanel's life who went by the name of Boy. When Boy came along, not only did he see CoCo for who she was; he also saw the greatness that was within her that would potentially become known to so many people worldwide. Boy fell in love with Chanel and he made a decision to invest in the value of what already pre-existed in her.

"It only takes one right being to see the worth and the value of your brand"

-ONLY VALUE INVESTS IN VALUE-

If someone does not know their worth they will not value yours, there has to be a level of already pre-existing understanding and knowledge. Don't allow others to lower you, because they failed to keep pursuing their own greatness. God's love and blessings are for us all.

Your brand will take you through doors, places, events, and higher levels that you use to just dream about. I have met so people just off of the fact that I known that I am great and I trust in who I am as a person, as a mother, as an entrepreneur, as a business woman, and as a brand.

CHAPTER

20

REACH YOUR OWN AUDIENCE

Where are the consumers?

Online, online, online!

If you have no website, blog, or some form of digital platform you literally have no business in today's society. Consumers are spending their time online. According to Nielson, 3 billion of the population is online. By 2019, women will control

$28 trillion annual consumer spending. As a mother I can attest to the fact that my children find at least 80% of what they desire me to purchase online first. This is where children are spending their free time; this is where they tell their parents to spend their free time.

85% of global consumers are using their mobile devices while watching TV

54% of the world's population in urban areas will have increase by the year of 2050 to 66% of the world's population

If you have a kids friendly business, make sure that kids are able to find you. They are the ones who influence their parents to buy. If you are a parent then you should know that it works. Today's kids are on these platforms:

1. Tumblr
2. SnapChat {Kids mode}
3. Instagram
4. YouTube
5. Kik
6. Ova

I remembered when the KD's released; my daughter literally went crazy over getting a pair. She had to have them, the price $119. She was sold on the idea that she needed them and she sold me on the idea that she wanted them. Children today want brands; they look for brands that are hot, new, and the latest. This is why it is so important to know your market, who you are marketing to, because it will determine your online time. You want to go directly to your market, all business owners hate wasting time. When you have lost time; you have lost money that is just the way that it is.

This is why it is so important to know your market, who you are marketing to, because this will determine how you spend your time while online. Ask yourself more questions:

1. Do you have products to offer children? When marketing to kids you have to be careful, because no one wants adults talking to their children. The safest way to do so is through sponsored advertising, digital flyers, YouTube videos, and online commercials. Or are you offering products to the adults?

2. What does your target market enjoy doing in their free time while online? Dating, chatting, meeting new people, shopping, or are they just looking to grow their network?

3. Are you looking to partner with others to start a new project?

4. Are you looking to attend events, model, or start an acting career?

5. Are you listening to music? Are your potential customers listening to music?

6. Are you producing music?

7. Are you marketing to readers, writers, or those who are in the process of writing?

The list goes on, the point is, *"Who are you looking to market your brand to and where are they spending their time?"* Once you find out who, what, when, where, and why, you want to know what is trending on social media. If you log onto your twitter account, type in the search #Trending topics You will see a list of currents trends listed to the left of the page and in the center you will see current conversations that are trending. You want to get involved in these conversations, they have listed different trends according to the currents events, holidays, politics, celebrity news, and brand launches.

Tweet moi → @mhumes #MoniBranding101 #OwnYourOwnBrand

Below is a screenshot of what it looks like when you search trending topics on twitter.

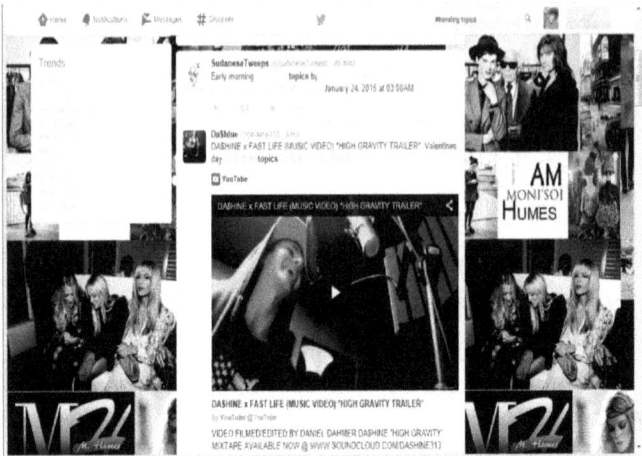

Hashtags play an important role in your online consumer engagement with your potential customers, fans, audience, or target market. Your intentions should be to build online relationships with individuals, brands, and companies that you want to do business with. I am not so sure if people even care about the trends, as much as they do to just be involved, and being a part of something huge. Trends are your chance to start an open discussion, start new business relationships, build rapport, and so forth. I am almost sure that when you use hashtags that consumers, fans, and friends are already using that your tweets become more apt to be retweeted or they will re-post what you posted.

When it comes to celebrities they almost always re-tweet when you send them a direct tweet. During the release of #WeddingRinger, which I attending the movie premiere, because I understand PR so I was invited. Kevin Hart re-tweeted every post that I tagged him in {328 Re-tweets in 2 days}. We help celebrities, brands, companies promote their projects and they know this, therefore they return the love.

The same applies when new TV shows are airing, major events, red carpet events, and product launches. Get involved in the conversation on twitter. Find hashtags that help promote your brand.

There are so many online communities that are available for different things; you just have to know what you are marketing and where these consumers are hanging out. Writers and readers are hanging out on Good Reads. Why? On Good reads you are able to have an Author's page, buy books, write reviews, and join other writers or authors communities. Also I love Style.com, this is a great place to see what is hot in the fashion industry, and also it gives you a chance to see what the consumers are interested in. Yahoo News is great as well, just do your research to find reliable sources.

Once you find out where the consumers are you want to know what is trending on social media.

Again Tweet moi @mhumes #MoniBranding101 #OYOB #PRPlan Tweet moi your questions and how you like my book on branding. I want to know how it is helping your #BrandCareer

It is important that while you are online that you engage with these individuals. If they follow you, take the time to check out their page, their service, or products. See what they are writing about, new topics, blog post, read some of their comments, and reply back to their comments, they just may be a future partner or customer, or even a future client. Keep your options open to full opportunity.

Find the trending hashtags that help promote your brand online. These are some of my favorites on Instagram @monisoihumes

#iammonisoihumes #iaminternational #MoniBranding101 #Dubai #DubaiNights #Fashion #FashionEditor #Paris #ParisNights #UAE #NewYork #NYC #Atlanta #Cali #LosAngeles #AmbassadorforGod #London #France #Italy #Luxury #Lifestyle #SoiLifestyle #LuxuryLifestyle #Starbucks #StarbucksObssessed #MercedezBenz #Writer #Author #Branding #FashionPhotography #Couturealist #HumesLuxuryIntl #Travel #LuxuryTravel #Entrepreneurs #Success100

#Embody-success-now #FashionBloggerChic #FairyTalePrincess #PRGoddess #MoniLovesIt #SoiLifestyle #SoiLifestyleTravel #PRPlan

Some brands use these for #instalikes #Instagram #ig #likeforlike #follow4follow #photography #contest #picoftheday #filter #nofilter

Via my agency: #RageBellaRa #RedCarpet @rbragency #Entertainment #Music #publicrelation #advertising #luxuryprboutique #celebrities #luxuryhotels #concerts

Via event promotion: #Vegas #NewYork #Atlanta #LosAngeles

Since I have found what hashtags that I love to use, when I post it gets me more likes than if I was to have no hashtags at all within my posts. Your hashtags will target only a specific audience. You can also go into your settings when you make a post on Instagram, it will post to Twitter, and Facebook. Why not kill 3 birds with one stone or market with one post? Lol. Also, Buffer is a great app for scheduling post. This app can be used for free, however it is limited. You can also purchase a paid subscription to preschedule more post with multiple accounts. Use this with caution, some of your followers on Instagram are different that the ones on your other networks. I use Instagram often, but I have learned that some post should only be for my Instagram followers. You don't want your target market to feel like you don't have the time to personally engage in conversing with them.

Your target market is the voice of your brand. You want to know your brand so well that attracting these individuals will be automatic. Your target marketing will be come in many ways to you:

1. A new friend

2. Counselor

3. Stylist or a barber

4. Membership of a new organization

5. Parent at a school meeting or student event

6. During shopping at a mutual market, boutique, salon, or a spa

7. New business Partner

8. Referral

9. A new site subscriber

Word of mouth is huge when it comes to promoting your brand. 90% of the individuals that have come to me as a client have been through the form of word-of-mouth referral. I do my best to treat others the best that I can, to inspire them, motivate them, and encourage them. I also know that by offering more to clients than what they are paying for is more memorable than anything. Take care of those who are also taking care of you. Don't de-value your customers, they are helping support your brand by being a client. Give your customers the value that they deserve.

This is how you turn customers into clients. Treat them with the same respect as your friend.- This is true value.

There is an old myth, *"Don't be close friends with those in whom you do business with,"* such as hang out with them or so forth. Now I know there are boundaries, however this is a part of relationship building. People do business with people who are like friends. Most business people don't have time for a personal life, they spend their free time with those in whom they do business with. They invite these same people to dinner parties, yacht parties, company events, and so forth. This is the best way for you to flow and operate.

The law or relativity-Nothing moves until you do.

CHAPTER

21

STRATEGY

You will learn that there is nothing in your life that just happens, everything happens for a reason. When you discover that the hardest part of releasing your brand is the part when everything around you is working to force the movement of your direction. While working on this project, this book, I was also was working on some things in my personal life. The birthing pains that I felt as I was delivering greatness unto myself, my family, and unto the people was very hard for me. I felt that I needed a coach to tell me that it was going to be ok, or that it would be better. It was then that I began to realize that my life was asking me to dig deeper within myself. I had to speak myself out of where I was.

You will feel as though no one understand when trials come your way, they just assume that you did something wrong this is not always true.

God just wants you to increase in strength and remove some people and individuals that are around you that mean you no good. It was discouraging and it added fuel to the fire. The less that I saw that no one was there to motivate the leader. I had to re-think with strategy, I thought back, then I remembered the person that inspired me years ago, so I text her.

The text read:

WHEN YOU REACHED HARD TIMES IN YOUR JOURNEY, WHAT DID YOU DO? IT SEEMS AS THOUGH I CONTINUED TO BE TESTED?

She told me that I had to get up every day and out loud just declare and decree affirmations until what I wanted manifested. Every day is not good even for successful individuals, but you must push forward.

When it is time to defeat your adversaries, you will need some level of understanding, and powerful warriors that are willing to go to battle with you and for your brand. What you are fighting for is ownership.

The average individual does not want to own up to anything let alone own, but to the individual that says there is more to me and that is why I desire ownership. They are bound to win. You have to adjust your strategy to fight for ownership and dominion.

Do not go into your business with no plan, let alone no strategy. The strategy is how you will overcome all that will come against your vision Don't listen to those who say they don't have a backup plan. The backup plan is the strategy to ensure that the plan works. You want the plan to work point blank. Save some of your energy for those who are going to fight against you, because it will be a low blow when those in whom you least expect hit you like they are your worst enemy. It will come from an unexpected place. I am telling you now, therefore prepare.

Individuals fold on you when it is time to put the strategy at work, if there is no strategy the plan will not work. Do not worry, let them fold, just be prepared again to work the strategy. You do not come this far into branding yourself or to be branded to lose your territorial rights. It is time to fight the good fight of faith. This is the point where some of your attacks will be not be seen. It will take faith to get you through this one.

Prepare to have a team of faith, who are prayerful, and strength filled warriors that will cover you through this entire season, and nothing will touch you. I am telling you it works. You should have a team of people for different seasons, attacks, and outside destructions. Individuals solve problems differently.

You need a team of individuals that are problem solvers. This is a part of your strategy. Companies that don't prepare for their enemies or attacks will fold. I have seen it with my own two eyes. Do not watch on the sidelines as the enemy comes to take over. Stand in your rightful place and do not move. See the salvation of God. Your opponent is not prepared for God to stand in vengeance against your enemies, but oh well. Either they join the team or move out of the way.

As God surrounds your life, your mind, your body, soul, spirit, your family, your home, your business, and your brand with a covering of pure omniscience power, your enemies will wonder, *"How in the world did you overcome everything that was thrown your way?"* No offense, but I worship a bad God. He protects me through any storm. Any storm.

What they did not expect, what I did not expect were the ones who did not help in the beginning would come in and fight my battles.

Step out the way meditate, pray, and get inside of you as you are only gaining access to a higher source of energy.

CHAPTER

22

THE POWER OF YOUR OWN TEAM

Rich people develop a team around them;
they do not do everything alone.

Building is one thing, building as a team is an entirely different thing, and understanding that there is power in team work is nothing but power itself. I have sat back and I have watched individuals that push me, motivate me, and inspire me. I have learned from them in many aspects. I have learned that some people possess an enormous amount of power that they just carry it with a lid on it. When you are in the process of building you will reach a phase of doing everything yourself, it is hard to avoid. This is how you learn all aspects of what you are doing and how to build it correctly, but you must also be very careful that you don't cross the line of getting comfortable with doing you. Leave room to allow others to come in and take over those positions this is not only how you will grow and elevate it is also how you will allow your team to grow together. There is power in oneness and there is also power in numbers, they both require unity, teamwork, and being on one accord as each individual must play their position. Successful individuals thrive off of money and power that is just the way that it is.

Focusing on your brand and increasing its power, you also will increase in your learning. Leaders fail because they fail to release power to those in whom they are leading. It is vital to have powerful team of players. You will never see a coach tell just the key players to work out; everyone on the team is required to put in the same time, energy, and the same effort. This is how they develop through the fundamental stages and also are able to keep up and maintain as they begin to grow to higher levels, winning locally, nationally, and winning championships.

In learning anything, there is and must be an understanding to the process of levels, as we all have heard several times that there are levels to this life. Levels are indeed a part of the process and it is very important to understand that everyone is not going to move with your brand as it increases in levels. The worst experience a person can experience is the desire to grow with the people that started with you, yet knowing that they are not elevating with you as your brand grows they will only keep you trapped in the last season of your life. If you allow this, your brand will face a dying out period. You don't want this to happen, you will begin to realize that the individuals that want you to stay here are only selfish and looking out for them.

Building is about teamwork, one thing about me is the fact that I want my entire team to be able to eat from what I bring to the table. It is only fair to expect them to have the same mentality. This is about growth, winning, and expansion. It is also about sacrifices, I have given up a lot of things that

I desired for the greater good, a bigger vision, the process, and the victory.

I am and I will continue to remain to be a huge advocate for team work makes the dream work. Working in the industry I have seen many individuals who are consumed with greed and they are constantly tearing down and re-building every year, because they don't see the value of what they have to offer.

Observe the individuals that you bring on board, know that there is something there that needs to be developed. You must also know if you are able to develop what is there. As a leader it is so important to have and develop the ability to bring out the greatness that is inside of the people who you are building with. They will appreciate you and your brand in the long run.

I have met several people that spoke greatness to me even when I did not see it in myself. They breathe life into my very existence. I will never forget those people, because they saw something I did not see, and they were not afraid to pull it out of me. Leaders know who has the want, need, and who has a pure desire to be become great. They see something that they have already experienced before they embraced their own greatness. Leaders will always desire to duplicate themselves.

CHAPTER

23

THE PR PLAN

Own your Own Brand

Now that you have discovered that what you have is so wonderful that the entire world wants a part of it, we must put together a PR Plan to put your brand out into the universe. The world is waiting to see what you are all about. They want to buy it. We know we need the exposure, but where do we start?

I mean let's be honest not everyone has the $3500 a month to hire a Publicist.

Our plan is to build and brand your brand in phases, work with what you have. Sometimes there are Publicist who are looking to get their agency off the ground. They are willing to offer small portions of services to help build you as a brand to gain you as a PR client; this is what I did for my clients. I understand how hard it is to get off the ground from 0 that is why I made it apart of my plan to just build with some partners that were willing to work with me. Just make sure that both parties are going to put in the work. You don't want to build relationships with individuals just to find out they didn't want to put the time and effort into building and promoting your project.

If you begin to view your relationship with your business partner the same way that you do your personal life you will look at things different. I know for me I hate to waste time, and God knows that I have. From my own personal experience I can attest that it is important to pay attention to specific qualities that can be promoted in your "publicity campaign." Make sure that whomever that you work with are flexible to making a few adjustments if necessary, this is all publicity.

There is nothing a Publicist can do with a client that won't show up, that will not listen, that will not learn, and look the part. This all goes back to look, learn, and listen. You must tear down the walls of any barriers, race, sex, age, religion, or even culture. You would be surprised how many people bring this negativity into the world of business and feel that it is ok. They desire for you to be bound by race, being a women, being a men, a certain religion, or a certain culture.

Know your brand, because if you are as I am #iaminternational then you cannot live with any boundaries that will keep you bound to one location, a certain group, or a certain skin color. Don't be given to ignorance, you are pushing your own brand.

Long before the push starts you want to keep a small notebook and you want to start to jot down names, companies, possible partners, and prices. This is so that when you are ready you can refer back to these items in your PR Plan.

Most PR Campaigns run for a 6-12 month period, some campaigns are not just for funds, some run campaigns to create exposure, and for the promotion of a new book release, a product launch, political election, fashion week, or an upcoming event. The worse thing that an artist or brand can do and many people do it, but you get on the phone and you contact a Publicist 2-3 months out from your launch date, and it is too hard for them to work in this small amount of time. Think about the time that you put into your project, give them the time to invest into their portion of their own baby project built around strategically pushing your campaign. This allows the space to help the client push their vision and get the desired exposure that is needed.

As you gather information, you want to start creating a list of reporters, local radio stations, podcast, and online blogs, bloggers, and online radio shows. You want to start engaging with individuals that can and have the power to help you put your name, your brand, and your company out there.

List of Publicity to-do-list

1. Create a media List

2. Create a list of events

3. Create a schedule of news release dates

4. Set a product launch date

5. Create a list of press run time for receiving pitches for magazines, some want pitches 6-12 months in advance, this is why you must be timely.

6. Schedule photo shoots / video shoots (This is for your content or your clients online content.)

7. Gather leads {Emails, phone numbers, and addresses}

8. Are there any speaking engagements that you can speak at? Write them down, along with their contact information, subjects, topics, etc...

9. Are there any network marketing companies that you can join as a vehicle to help open up your network and more brand opportunities? Write them down, pick one, or create your own network marketing or affiliate system.

You have some brands that are so involved into what they are creating that they are planned 5 years out in detail, of course with the understanding that there will be adjustments made to the plan. You want to ensure that you are able to connect with partners, team members, and potential sponsors.

Trust that no one wants to be involved with a brand with no PR plan. It is not happening.

You want to do some research on the following:

1. Writing a great pitch letter

2. Creating a great Sponsorship package

3. Know the company's brand that you want to partner with [Culture, Executive Summary, Mission Statement, Staff Members, and the events that they are currently involved in]

Ask yourself:

1. What value can you add to what they already have in existence?

2. Are you involved in any charity events or 501 3c's this is always great for publicity? It is a plus to always give back.

3. What is it about your brand that stands out?

4. Can you connect and partner with other brands that do the same thing that you do? Successful brands are not afraid to partner with similar brands, they lack intimidation.

Take all these things into consideration when working on your PR plan and remember that there are many sites that are out there that are available to help you.

CHAPTER

24

OWN THE MOMENT TO LIVE FIERCE

You have finally reached that moment, your product is complete and available to the marketplace, you have been pushing your campaign, and promoting like hell. Now it is time to show up. There are some great brands out here, but some of them never show up to be seen by the consumers.

Companies, sponsors, and partners want to see the person that they are investing in, they want to see your face, and they want to communicate with you face to face.

The truth is that yes, everyone is online, but do not forget that face to face communication still matters to those who are relevant. If they cannot ever see you in person you just may not even exist. It is so easy to go online and create a profile that even robots do so, this is why it is vital to let people see you, meet you, and get to know you. It is again your opportunity to build up rapport and to give them knowledge of your brand.

You will need to create a list of events for your PR Plan. Once you create a list of events everything in hell will try to keep you from showing your face, why? Because your enemies know that the hard work has already been done, once you show your face-Your brand goes from being behind the scenes to being in the spotlight. *The spotlight is your time for you and your brand to become one and shine.*

You only live once, you might as well do it big whether you are a promoter, artist, fashion designer, fashion photographer, blogger, entrepreneur, makeup artist, model, DJ, stylist, or Creative Director you have only one time to do it right.

There are several events that you may want to put on your list of events to attend.

- Grammy Awards

- BET Live Experience

- MTV Awards

- Oscars

- New York Fashion Week

- Paris Fashion Week

- Mercedes Benz Fashion Week

- A3C Festival

- BET Music Matters

- LA Times Book Festival

- Teen Choice Awards

- High-end Runway Shows

Once you get on the invite list, add these to your PR Calendar. This is great publicity! Look for events that are in your genre. Your plan is to go there to network, take some great Instagram pics, and build up your resources.

Also look into joining different associations and organizations, they will inform you of upcoming events that are taking place, some of which they may even be hosting. I am a member of the National Black MBAA, when they had their conference-it was immediate access for me as a member. Events that are hosted by a large organization are great for publicity. Events that have over 15,000 attendees are great places to go and network, politic, and advertise your product.

Think big! Think huge! Keep your mind open for the flow of publicity, publicity, and more publicity. You need it for your brand's awareness.

When you reach the stage when you are putting your brand out and you begin marketing, you will hear "No" sometimes, but do not take it as an option. You have to convince others that you are adding value to their brand as well. No from another business owner only means that they need a little more convincing or this is a new territory for them. **You have to be willing to help some business owners run hard in their own business**.

Remember cast down all thoughts of what you were taught and how you were taught. If your brand is going to do this then you must be open to the fact that you a bringing game to the table. There are some businesses that you are going to call that will need you to help them to understand how they can take what they do to the next level.

Talk to people in charge, managers turn down business for the business owner so contact the owners or the ceos. I have experienced this personally, get the owner on the phone. Sometimes you have to go over the Managers head, because they don't understand the fabric of what it takes to own a business. They come in to run what is already in existence. Don't shoot yourself in the foot when a manager tells you no, their power is limited when they are not open to increase.

When you are bringing a new product to the table that can advertise or launch their business to the next level and they respond, "No," with no option for you to send them a layout or set up a meeting. Fire them. They are destroying business for the owner. If they are turning down your free advertising, then they are turning away business for the company.

Start operating in full ownership, start firing individuals that are in your brands way and in the way of another business owner's success. We are all in business to succeed. Sometimes you have to help other business owners see the fact that they have poor management on deck.

You would be surprised how many business owner hire managers off their talk game, and you will also be surprised how many mangers talk others out of doing business with you. **If you are in a Management role and you are reading this, open your mind up for opportunity before you get fired.**

A business sole intentions are to produce profit once it opens; yes we start off with just passion, yet the goal once we open it is to produce profit. The owner has a right to know if their management is causing them to lose revenue. If you were hired due to a friendship; do your friend a favor increase their business or move out of the way. Besides every day you are coming in with the mentality on how you can do what they do and even better. This is unacceptable. **There is no time for jealousy on the clock.**

Brands open up the doors for other brands, other companies, celebrities, NBA players, and NFL players, stars, and so on to shine. If you do not know this your brand won't live, in fact it will die in vain. #monibranding101

Your goal is to prepare for each and every event like it is a special occasion-Treat it as such. Be prepared to show up in your best. Once you arrive, own the room. I don't care who hates it. I don't care who does not like you, because eventually they will be hiring your brand to represent them. Be open to being a host.

Once you demand all attention when you walk in a room, the person who is in charge will want you to do it again. A celebrity is nothing more than a brand that owns the spotlight. This is why one day Kim Kardashian was organizing Paris Hilton closet and the next day she was famous. No one knew who Kim was. I didn't and I

Celebrity-a brand that owns the spotlight

am sure many others can attest to this same thing. Once she was noticed by paparazzi, the people chose to make her famous. Everyone says it was her sex tape with Ray J, but was it? Kim K was branding herself and she gave a rat's ass who liked it. The truth is the truth. The more you talk about Kim, the more she gets paid. That is how publicity works. This is how brands shine. It may hurt your feelings from some of the things that you hear, but then you check your bank account, your lifestyle, and your status, and you presume back to what you were doing.

The media is trained to predict stories according to the people's reaction. This book is not for the people, it is for brands who are looking to go beyond the position of normal to the position to stand out, stepping out, and living a life in boldness.

This is why social media is so popular. It has given individuals all over the world the opportunity to shine. When you give opportunity to people they take it. The only people mad about the individuals taking this opportunity are the ones who didn't have the platform or the ones who were afraid to operate in greatness on their own.

Understand this though, those who had to get out into the streets, show up here and there, and knock on the doors of the media companies have a higher knowledge of what it takes to make it and survive. Today people operate on social media and they are still broke, because they have nothing to offer but the fact that they are in love, drunk, just got married, or some bad drama going on. Don't get me wrong these things sell, but when it comes down to business, a business owner wants to know what exactly you have to offer to them.

Celebrities, brands, athletes don't sell these things, they over stand the relevance and the value of their own privacy. The more you hold out, the more you get. Stop selling your life, start selling your brand-there is a difference.

My mission has always been to produce product, inventory, and creating assets. At the end of the day this is where your profit is. The world is in a reality phenomenon and when the show is washed up they have nothing to show for it. Why? The brand that put the show on the air is done with them. Brands produce reality shows, movies, short films, record labels, clothing lines, and books, because they want to be in control of the direction of their brands success. When a person is on a reality show and they understand branding, they plan, expect, create, and get more gigs.

Real brands do not shine until they have been processed. #monibranding101

    Once you go through the process you are able to walk into the room with the heart of a lion or a lioness and be fierce. Don't make the mistake that many make dimming your lights, because the world can't handle your greatness. There is a superstar in you that screaming to come out.

CHAPTER

25

OWN THE BOSS IN YOU

Boss up!

There is a god or goddess in you, waiting for you to explore, and now that you have an incredible plan you need to embrace what is in you and begin the process of possession and manifest that in which you desire. You knew that one day that it was inevitable, that you would be asked to walk in those boss shoes or that you would have to wake up and step into them your damn self. There is no time like the present to do so. Being the boss is a huge responsibility, however you have more than enough tools to be exactly who God created you to be without the worry of what others want you to be. Tell those who have an issue with your greatness to, "*Fall back.*"

Stop working to please others and work.

The greatest question anyone has ever asked me was, *"Are you going to do what I want you to or else I am leaving you?"* Well, deuces, because I love myself for who I am, compromising that for anyone was not an option for me. What made it such a great question was the fact that it told me who I needed to kick to the curve. I refuse to bow down to powerless beings when I knew that I on my own am a #powerhouse. You are a #powerhouse, let no one tell you any different.

The world will do its best to control the route that you travel and that is a hard thing for you to deal with. It was hard for me to lose some of the people I lost due to their inability to handle my growth. The thing is that successful individuals do not change, the people who are in their life just change how they feel about them. I take that back the only change successful people make is growth and development and the people around them decide that they rather not grow with them. You want to stay focused, meditate, and pray daily. Remember why you started every day. Make it apart of your business to focus on your goals and affirmations to keep yourself motivated in the vision that God gave you not people. It will carry you through the heaviest days, because this is only the beginning as you go forward you will be given more responsibilities. You may feel like you want to quit on your brand, but keep pushing. You will feel like there is so much coming against you. There will be days you will feel like you can't handle it, but repeat your daily affirmations whatever you have written down in writing claiming it to come to forward.

You must do this regardless of how you feel. Trust me, if you don't you will end up like many individuals who get in the industry or higher positions and get addicted to bad habits-cocaine, alcohol, sex, pills, or whatever it is that is out there. Being successful can be stressful if you do not have a natural stress reliever. Meditation and prayer helps me to stay at peace.

I am so thankful to God that my brand is bigger than my storm and that I am able to tell you that your brand is bigger than your storm. Everything in this world tried to destroy me and when I felt like I had enough I received a phone call from a very special and important person to me. On this important day, these words changed my life.

He said to me, *"You know you are very special. An individual can tell the day that they meet you, but as special as you are there are agents that assigned to destroy you, and keep you off course for as long as they can. You are allowed to have this day to be human, however remember that people log online just to read your motivational post. You are awesome. Keep being awesome. Go to sleep tonight a human, but tomorrow wake up being who you know yourself to be."* Van Johnson

This was very powerful to me, I felt like before then that the affliction was too much. I wanted to just go to sleep and lay there for a while. I wanted to wallow in my pain, in my tears, and in my heart ache, but because my vision was huge-I had to go to sleep and wake up powerful.

I had to not question my brands story or my storm. Some people actually planned storms to get my attention, throw me off course, and to keep me from focusing. I knew that God would remain in control, however as a human I felt that my storms were too real. I wanted them to go away. I did not want to even tell anyone that I was going through anything. They would not understand at least this is what I thought to myself and the few I told looked over the fact that I was feeling something that terrified me.

This is when I realized that it is dangerous being a boss, because human expectations are thrown out of the window. No matter what you do from this point you must remember that it is the price that you pay to lead. Your bad days will be few compared to the many days of blessings that God will bestow through you and upon your life.

If you are a leader then you know what I mean when I say, "*I wish that I could be human.*" You understand the demand, the mantle, and the crown that is upon your life.

It does not matter who feels you are not great, you are. Beyond being a brand, you must remain motivated to live the best life ever as you.

People will walk away. People did walk away from me. They thought that I would stop fighting, they had no knowledge of my will power. They had no knowledge of my brand's power.

I knew a long time ago that I would move mountains; walk through many doors that were closed to others. I knew what I knew. I also knew that I had to see the individuals who were for me good and bad.

When someone is for you they will stick it out with your brand –good and bad. Shout out to my promoter for sticking it out with my brand. He did not go against the vision to create something else. He remains loyal to the purpose. You must always remember to give praise where praise is due.

A boss will have certain traits that must remain respected:

- Loyalty
- Integrity
- Patience
- Tenacity
- Endurance

Once you see these traits, know that eyes have not seen, ears have not heard of the glory that is in these individuals. You will see miraculous things happen for these individuals. As a boss you remain faithful and to continue to pour into and look out for those who look out for you, because they are few and hard to find.

STATEMENTS OF TRUE LEADERS:

1. They are investors of time.

2. Dedicators to passion

3. Givers to greatness

4. Pushers past pain.

These individuals have experienced something so painful in life before you met them that they refuse to turn back to anything outside of hard work. When you find the boss in you, respect the bosses around, and learn to build together. Cross the bridge together. Fly across the globe together.

I use to be an advocate of these words, "I am so alone." We are never alone; we are always in the presence of absolute greatness.

Make a personal note of those who see and know you and your brand, acknowledge them. #monibranding101

Being a boss is the accepting of the crown of your glory.

PR Goddess

CHAPTER

26

LOVE THE BRAND YOU ARE IN

I AM: Public Figure

MY CAREER: Agent, Author, Blogger,
                     Coach, & Writer, Fashion &
                     Style, Designer, Social & PR
                     Goddess, & living the
                     luxurious *Soi Lifestyle*

> "WHEN YOU CAN SEE IT,
> YOU CAN BECOME IT, &
> THEN YOU CAN HAVE IT"

IAM INTERNATIONAL

Atlanta Dubai Beverly Hills
Hollywood Italy London Los
Angeles Miami New Orleans
NYC Paris

Great individuals usually have some type of great inspiration. When you see yourself from where you have been to where you are going it changes things. You want to have a vision board for your vision of success then you want to lay out a vision board of where you started to monitor the tasks that you have already accomplished along the way.

Now that you have created the life, the brand, and the vision that you desired you need to just sit back and fall in love with what you have created. Love is a beautiful thing especially when you have labored through time, talent, gifts, and passion.

It is often that we get so caught up that we forget the passion, and the fire that had us lit up like fireworks that were just waiting to explode. When you put love into you brand it helps you to deliver a message.

Make sure the statement that your brand will always be remembered by, make it from the heart. Do not second guess your hearts message. While building my brands-love was my storm, having to overcome that emotional distress when things were not going my way was way too much, but I had to push hard.

Stop looking at those that are around you, the blessings that you desire are within you. What your neighbor, friend, family members have ownership of has nothing to do with what God has for you. God is the ultimate giver of life. He vowed to make your name great, therefore making your brand phenomenal.

My Goal

"Create a lifelong brand."

Lifelong brands have 501 3c's named after them, bridges, holidays, streets, boulevards, museums, collections, clothing lines, days, months, and even parks. This is territorial branding when people have fallen so much in love with your brand that they begin to push your name into new territory. This is a must, especially if you are big thinker. Be grand! Be bold! Be phenomenal! Why not? You are not just a brand you are a boss.

Rocking my boss attitude was wonderful, until yep until. It was a Saturday night and I received a phone call. OK. I am so not ready for by the way, but hey I am a business woman and a boss at that. But, no this Bit** didn't. As I am on the phone listening, not liking what I am hearing, so I just sit the phone on the counter while being on speaker. The woman goes on and on, I won't mention who she is, because that would be unprofessional. She began to tell me all the things that I needed to do from the way that I needed to look, what I should say, how I should say, to who I needed to hang around with, and who I needed to cut off, and even what man I needed to be with and not. I knew that in the professional world that there should have been a way better approach than the one that she was taking then she responds and says, "*Take the negativity that I am giving you and do what you are supposed to do and give your business up right now and just focus on what we have going on.*" This is the moment when the PR Goddess disappears from within me and says,

-Fuc* Publicity

This is the moment when I realized that it is possible to give away a huge part of your life to help make a difference in the lives of the people. Immediately I reverted back into my boss mode, "*Someone needs to fire this woman I thought to myself.*"

However my reaction, my response was much different. Look I was chosen to lead to get a job done, there are several things that are unorganized and no one else wanted to get the job done. Now I sent over a list of tasks by email detailing the things that needed to be completed. We can talk all day, *"How about we take action to get these things done?"* Now she could not have heard me, because she continued to go on and on before the phone just lost signal and hung up. I guess the vibrations that she was sending were so negative that she was cut her off. Thank God.

Be careful who you spend time with over the phone. The phone sends different vibrations through it, this is how sometimes when we hang the phone up that either negative or positive energies have transmitted to you.

I apologize to those who are reading, I love PR. It is not a bad thing, this woman just had a hard life and a hard day and she needed someone to take it out on and she chose to dish it out to me. She chose to treat me like someone was obviously treating her.

No guts, no glory is what this woman obviously felt.

This happens a lot in the world of public relation, the industry, government, politics, society, and in organizations-any time someone feels like they can badger you, bully you, or enforce some type of control over you, watch them very closely. They are usually filled with rage, jealousy, torment, and they have an enormous fear of any change.

I did not fear this woman's words rising up against me. It should be expected to be upsetting for those who have done things one way their entire life when someone younger comes in and says, *"Lets' do things differently now, the old way is no longer working."*

Once you recognize the individuals that are attacking, know that they are attacking your love for what you do, not your leadership. If they can get you to stop loving what you do there is no need for your leadership.

-Love is weird like that.-

Love has this uncanny ability to make you feel wonderful to deal with the unexpected, to turn your life upside down. Yet it carries you through the roughest storms in your life.

I know that I am not in the room with you, but raise your hands if you can relate to this feeling of mere passion, desire, and you are willing to fight for something, or someone that you love.

Love is my brands story.

Where you have fought the hardest is where God will give you the most increase. It may not feel like it, however when rain comes it does a few things.

1. It creates moisture

2. It washes away dirt

3. It causes growth in plants, food, and trees.

Rain is natural, so is the thunder storms; this is why when there are bad weather storms, such as tornadoes, hurricanes, and volcanoes they are all labeled as natural disasters. The reason being is that there are just some things that you have to learn to just flow freely.

My Aunt use to say when I was a little girl that when it was storming outside that we should be still and let God work. I don't believe that was just physical, it is also spiritual. It takes time and patience to allow natural things to process and flow. This applies to the life of our brand, by allowing love to continue to flow it allows you to just keep trusting in the God within to keep making what seems to be the least among you the greatest amongst you.

Owe a man nothing, but to love him.-God

CHAPTER

27

MONI BRANDING 101

Branding is about making your own mark, telling your own story, and sharing your own brand with the specific target market.

Plan to take action!

Work the plan until it looks, feels, and sounds like you want it to. It is your name on the line. You have to be willing to help some business owners run the race that was set before them. If you are in a Management role and you are reading this, open your mind up for opportunity before you get fired. There is no time for jealousy on the clock.

Brands open up the doors for other brands, other companies, celebrities, and NFL players, NBA players, superstars, and so on to shine. If you do not know this your brand won't live, in fact it will die in vain.

Real brands do not shine until they have been processed. Most individuals miss out on their greatest achievements simply, because they are afraid to go through the process. Why fear being the greatest you ever? You only live once, therefore spend it doing the things that you love doing. Don't waste time doing what others want you to do, it will only set you back in the progress of your own success.

Make a personal note of those who see, know you, and your brand, acknowledge them.

Trust what you put out there or don't put it out there. If you don't believe in your brand, product, or services-no one else will.

Be open to moving out of your comfort zone. Every successful brand must be open to becoming international.

Partner only with brands that can be identified with your brands story.

Make your entire request known unto God. In business all request are handle by the order in which they are received, if you are not connected to the source, to the guide in which you came from-your brand will be lost.

Keep your "brand" moving forward at all times. Consumers identify with brands that are moving through the cycle, growth, and the maturity of its life cycle. These are great signs that your brand is connecting with its audience.

Researchers become experts.

Experts are marketers.

Marketers know PR.

I put so much time and effort into building my brand through writing, blogging, releasing content, social media marketing, and attending as many events as possible to network. I knew that if I did enough online that others would be able to Google me and find me easily. The internet is all about others having the ability to log online and find you and your brand without them having to look all over the place. The same effort that you would put into finding a great location put in placing your brand online.

Make sure that you are willing to put and place as much energy and effort as possible in your brand. Do not get behind on what you are doing for no one, unless of course you are led by the spirit of God or a spiritual guide. We don't always see things coming our way, sometimes God uses others to guide us along the way. Stay open to change while you are marketing your unique PR Plan.

A list of great marketing tools:

1. Get Response-leads, emails on automatic

2. Join by Text

3. Google Analytics

4. Constant Contact

5. Bitly-Shortens links

6. Buffer-An app that syncs with your social media platforms and allows you to schedule post; also

makes post suggestions for twitter post, and it shortens all links before making post.

7. Hoot Suite-syncs with social media platforms and allows you to schedule post.

8. Wordpress-a great blogging platform that helps you promote your brand while also getting leads.

9. You are your greatest marketing assets. Get up and get out and market you. The people want to know who you are.

10. Kick-starter-Run your campaigns here and raise capital for your project.

11. Create an E-book to promote your business.

12. Give something away on your website for FREE.

13. Hire interns for a probationary period with the option to work a permanent position with your company.

14. Offer incentives to your staff and team members.

When you are in love with your brand and you push it constantly, so many others will also fall in love with your brand. Consumers are just waiting for the opportunity to connect with others who are doing and living the lifestyle that they wish that they had the guts to live.

CHAPTER

28

BE A MOGUL

"Eye made it"

When you reach a level in your career that no one expected you to reach you should be extremely proud of yourself, because what it means is that the next level that you face you can also conquer it.

What I love most is that people gave up, quit, and thought I would not make it, however when God puts his stamp on your name and your brand the only thing that you can do is make it.

The hardest part of becoming and embracing my own greatness was dealing with my own heart. "I am a heart breaker." Speaking from the sense of giving too much of myself, of my heart too fast, that when he is ready I am done. Most people don't give or know how to give to receive greatness. I go into relationships and business ventures with 100% of myself. I am a sprinter by nature and heart.

Being in the industry you have to know what you want, who you are, and how you want it or you will become a heart breaker. My life lives in infinite time, however I hate to waste it, this has to be like this for me. Relationships can make or break your career in the industry, think that it is a game. It does not matter which side that you are on-male or female if that person does not have the DNA makeup, structure, and strength of a #mogul they won't survive you. There is nothing worse that striving for more while being with someone who is comfortable with where they are. I could not see myself being with someone who just wants things to be one way all the time.

Now don't get me wrong I am a Capricorn, stability is a must, as well as setting a solid foundation. I just mean from the aspect we should always strive for excellence, to reach higher heights, and to do more. When you finish one goal, set another one, as an entrepreneur I live off of this. I may set a goal on Monday and complete it in 2 days, this means that I need to set another one. Goals are mini milestones to achieving the bigger picture.

Moguls are planners, thinkers, innovators, and more than that they don't stop going in. They build in steps and when they master it, they create something else to master.

Another-Moni Goal

{Infiltrate the market with the Moni'soi Humes brand.}

I am spoiled, I want what I want, but I work to live in the boss shoes that I live in. I didn't care how hard my journey was, my life had to become exactly what God wanted it to be. God gives an anointing to each of us to do something unique with our life and it is up to you whether you live that life or not.

Network your market.

If you are going to be in the industry, network your ass off. I don't care who tells you not to, or who tells you to chill out. "Do You"-Russell Simmons

Simmons is a mogul that we all know of, he set out to do what he does, and he does just that. He is not concerned with a stigma of how he should be; he became exactly what he saw, because he made a choice to do so. Everything for him is about enlightenment, peace, and unity. Once you make the time to allow these things to shine through you, the limitless is bound to happen for you. The universe is a space filled with nothing but opportunity for you to expand and all you have to do is to be open to living with a supernatural power to create, build, and live the life that you choose to live. The life already chose you. All you have to do is be open to accepting that life back into your space.

I remember an art teacher that I had once for a drawing course as his words were so powerful, "*You have to be accountable for the space that you take up in this universe. If you do nothing with it, then you waste it.*"

This stuck with me and it still is with me. I know that what you don't apply, you throw it away.

Your gift turns to garbage when you allow it to just sit still idol. You know you have a gift, yet you care less of the greatness that it is capable of. You are happy just knowing that you have it, well that is not enough. If you do not do anything to keep what you have, you are bound to lose it. I apologize for being the one to give you this bad news; however the truth is the truth.

Put your brand out there, this is publicity. Be proud of the news that you are about to share with the world. You are just giving birth to a seed that you carried in your spirit. Have a launch party for your product, brand, or a new company launch. Don't fear the reaction of the people; it is all good for your brand.

Moguls are fearless, bad in their boss shoes, and more than able to handle the position that they stand in. They are leaders who are born, with the goal to develop what is already there. Although moguls are leaders they hire leaders so they can remain Boss. Sometimes we confuse the two, but moguls all experience the same feeling of being alone while their team is playing together. There is nothing worse than being on a team and you are the only one who is playing, this is when I realized that I was not meant to be on the team. I was soon to realize that I was to coach the team.

It takes a lot of energy from a coach to make sure that your team stays motivated. People on the outside looking in don't realize that you are working on high levels to stay focused on your dreams, goals, mission, and vision.

When you are building there will be a lot of people that will be sent your way just to become a distraction. There will be situations that will come to try to sidetrack you from winning. Elevate your levels of energy continuously because you are closer to yet another victory and your team is about to win.

It is so exciting when you can visualize this greatness that is in you, when you realize that the god that is in you is performing your own miracles. As you move in this level of faith, God matches what is in you and surrounds you with everything that you have ever imagined. You are a powerful being. You are a powerful brand.

I want you to take this energy, this motivation, and turn the hell up on the world. While they are watching you anyway, you might as well put on a good ass show.

You didn't put in all the hard work for no reason; your brand deserves the celebration. Have your publicist type up a press release, set up a brand launch party, private movie screening, or listening party. She or he is already equipped with the marketing weapons to take your brand to the next level and show its beauty to the entire world if that is what you want for them to do.

Next your publicist will send your launch out to the media, set up your interviews, and get you the direct exposure that you desire.

In conclusion, do not allow anyone to hinder you. They don't even have that type of power unless it is given to them. You are only hindered by not having a PR Plan to refer to.

Now that you have read the PR Plan, it is time to get busy owning your own brand.

CHAPTER

29

WHAT INSPIRED THE PR PLAN?

Rage Bella Ra-RBR PR & Advertising Agency

The meaning of the name came to me, the company was shown to me to be a place, a haven, and a home for passion, beautiful entrepreneurs who understood culture and fighting for something greater than their right now as a brand. A new

WallStreet! Individuals that have to have it {Rage}.
The Ra' was revealed to me. It is Egyptian for the
sun god of Ancient Egypt.

What makes Rage Bella Ra' so unique as a
company is the fact that as the Founder I understood
how hard it is to just start, operate, & earn capital
for your business. What is even more difficult is the
fact that most entrepreneurs have a poor network,
poor support system, & a lack of resources. Today
in our society network marketing is a very huge
opportunity that exists for many entrepreneurs;
however on the other end most entrepreneurs don't
start their own company due to the lack of funds
amongst other sources. As an entrepreneur I made a
decision to change the path by allowing "bosses" to
partner with RBR and operate through a system of
branding their own company.

When you have an entrepreneurial spirit it is so
easy to become involved with network marketing.
Let's face it the opportunity is there, as well as the
need to invest. I stood in those shoes several times
which led me to the decision to help entrepreneurs
start their business under the umbrella of RBR with
"no initial investment" as majority network
marketing companies' offer.

As I began to strategically placing the pieces of the puzzle together I began to see my heart for others more than anything. My purpose in life is to help others fulfill their purpose, push their own brand, and focus on the objective. When you can visualize your success, lay it out, and don't get discouraged. Do not give up or give in. Others will fight against you, try to stop, but know that it is your enemies' job to keep you on your toes, either you get knocked out or you rise up and win.

Every day you should rise to win. I knew from my experience of what I was capable of, I was building people, branding them, and pushing them without even knowing it.

Other people had to show me that one of the females that I was pushing was leaving me behind while she was using me and my resources to come up. It was so natural for me to push people to be as great as they could be. I have always been the type of person in business that would not take no for an answer. All things are possible when you know who you are.

When I made it up in my mind that there was more to me and where I was, I knew that I had to make it my business to do what was natural for me for a living.

Waking up around 3 am in the mornings thinking about success, and the possibilities of what I could do next, and adding more task to the list when I completed the previous list. Pushing, because there was no longer anything behind me, everything behind me had already pushed me forward.

The greatest gift you can give yourself is to live the life that you desire to live. I was inspired to start Rage Bella Ra to create an umbrella that would deliver a unique message to all that it represented. I thought how intelligent to create a company and hire my own company to represent my own brand. All that I create had to find a home under its own umbrella's that all were created by my own entities.

I learned a valuable lesson through my own trials to not be so willing to put yourself to the side to help others unless you have been guided by God to do so. Let people know up front that it takes such effort to move forward in business with you. I was so excited that I literally was giving away my talent, giving away my own blessings, and I was eager to do so. I had to learn that although it is a leader's job to help others that those individuals must be willing to pay the price to be helped.

We all pay a price to be successful, whether we are training to run a marathon, staying up late hours in the night to finish that big project, or traveling from state-to-state, or country-to-country; we are up to do what must be done. We understand that if we don't pay the price for success, that someone else will come along and pay it for us.

The same goes when hiring a team that consists of a Publicist, Management, Promoters, Photographers, Marketers, Stylist, Fashion Designer, Musicians, Engineers, Producers, and all the other resources that you need to be successful. My personal decision is to surround myself with business minded individuals. I don't spend much time with people who are not money focused, business oriented, politicking, fashion related, music related, or in the profession that I am in. This is "What it takes." In my other book, "*Success is what you make it,*" Chapter 5 speaks on "What it takes," for you to be successful. Most people are not willing to do what needs to be done in order to elevate higher, make sure that you are not one of those individuals.

In conclusion, the PR Plan is my way of saying it is not too late to put a plan together, get out there, and run the race that God set before you with endurance. There is a hustler in you that wants to take your brand to the next level, either you agree with it or you move the hell out of everyone's way. Trust that you have the power to shine, create, and build a lifelong brand. Don't be afraid of the reaction or response of others, just be great!

ACKNOWLEDGEMENTS

People who know who you are will never do anything to keep you from moving forward in your own brand.

I can do all things. →**God**

I am royalty→ Sarah & Al Humes {Grandparents}

I am a private person→ Parents

Mompreneur →My beautiful children, royalty

My strive for excellence →Marylyn Hopkins {Auntie}, Louisiana

All of you are my foundation, my rocks.

My business hustle →Cash, Queens, NY

{Code you must survive, tell no one I mean no one what you are doing}

Industry hustle, operations of think tanks for fashion industry →Tye, Bronx, NY

Intelligence "Think 3 seconds before you speak, then speak with intelligence." Government contractor, who secures bids for $100,000 and higher

Female bosses *"Keep God first and everything else will follow"* Pamela Hand

Private business *"Life is a game; you just have to know how to play it."*→Ms. J

Soul watchers → Grandmother, Mom, Spiritual Mom

Much respect to my spiritual guide to living an infinite life Master teacher, Masonry, Culture of Egyptian Moor→Tony Mc Creary

Jason -S/O to a BF for life, You spoke life to moi in a place that I did not see myself when you said, *"You are the next La La."* Luv you dearly! My #rideordie

Rest in peace! The man that showed me my own roots →Mr. Lacey Calhoun-EL

Thanks to Leon Carbon for the beautiful images of moi for The PR Plan. You captured me effortlessly. I truly love your work & your continued support of this journey.

Thanks to my team. You will always be appreciated by moi. Luv you with the upmost!

Tiffany Terrell of TTC Consulting, I could not and would not have embraced the PR side of moi without God using you to show moi that vibrant light. Thanks lady, for the luv from one strong woman to another.

MY EDUCATION

Master Cosmetology	Graduated May 1999, Middle GA Technical College
Fashion Retail Management	Art Institute of Atlanta, GA
Fashion Merchandising	Academy of Art University, California
Favorite Courses	Management
	Fashion Marketing
	Consumer Motivation
	Fashion Journalism

CONFESSION OF A PR GODDESS

I KNEW THAT I MADE IT WHEN...

As a woman I spent a lot of time organizing, building, and doing my damn best to be pleasing to my family, loved ones, and those close to moi. No matter how hard that I worked at being better it was not until I realized that I needed to shine for moi, no one else. I woke up one day I I felt absolutely no concern about what anyone else thought about my success or my failures. I knew that whether I failed or succeeded that it did not matter to anyone as much as it did to me. I reached a place where I did not care anymore. I did not become heartless, but I could not care less of what others wanted me to be, or how they wanted me to do things.

When you reach a place in your career with this attitude you have indeed arrived to a higher level in your career as a mogul, a brand, and a powerhouse. My reason for building an empire changed, I needed to know of my own ability to build what I saw. I needed to prove to myself that I was able. I no longer needed anyone to validate any type of approval for me to do that.

I embraced the PR Goddess that I am & that I was born to be, to live in love, peace, truth, freedom, and justice.

ABOUT THE AUTHOR

MONI'SOI HUMES

INTERNATIONAL BRAND

Born in 1979, in Ouachita Parish, Louisiana, raised in a small home in the country side of Epps, Louisiana with grandparents-Sarah & Al Humes. Graduate of Master Cosmetology program and studied at the Academy of Art University for Fashion Merchandising.

Humes grew up reading and turning the pages of Vogue and Elle magazines looking for the latest luxury brands, checking out the fashion ad campaigns, the newest collections, & beauty trends. Today she combines her love for family, being a mom, life, beauty, fashion, lifestyle traveling, and writing to living her dreams to the fullest. Coach, Designer, Brand Consultant and Author of Success is What You Make it, Founder of Luxury PR Boutique-RBR PR & Advertising Agency, Humes Luxury *Intl*. along with many other of her boss endeavors. Currently she is residing in the US.

Monisoihumes.com

ADDITIONAL LINKS

PERSONAL BLOG

iammonisoihumes.wordpress.com

SUCCESS BLOG

success100campaign.wordpress.com

Fashion, luxury blog

www.couturealistdeluxe.com

Luxury PR Boutique
rbragency.com

REFERENCES

(n.d.). Retrieved 02 19, 2015, from Merriam Webster
   Dictionary: http://www.merriam-webster.com/
   dictionary/belief

(n.d.). Retrieved 02 19, 2015, from Merriam Webster
   Dictionary: http://www.merriam-webster.com/
   dictionary/know

Brands, T. W. (2014, November). *http://www.forbes.com/*
   powerful-brands/list/. Retrieved January 22, 2015,
   from Forbes, Fact Set: http://www.Forbes.com

Chanel, C. (n.d.). Retrieved 03 09, 2015, from Pintrest: https://
   images.search.yahoo.com/images/
   view;_ylt=AwrB8pMauv1UqVEA2rmJzbkF;_ylu
   =X3oDMTIzbjk1amg5BHNlYwNzcgRzbGsDaW
   1nBG9pZANiYmY0M2ZkM2YxOTM0ZDQwO
   DQ4ZTdmMjY2YmFiMGEyMARncG9zAzEwB
   Gl0A2Jpbmc-?.origin=&back=https%3A%2F
   %2Fimages.search.yahoo.com%2Fyhs%2Fsearch
   %

Emerson, M. (2014, April 29). *http://www.inc.com/*
   theupsstore/the-five-ps-of-marketing-product-
   place-promotion-price-and-profit.html. Retrieved
   Feb. 16, 2015, from INC.: www.inc.com

Godin, S. (2007). In S. Godin, *Permission Marketing* (p. 256).
   Pocket Books; New edition edition.

http://www.forbes.com. (2014, 04 18). Retrieved 02 17, 2015,
   from Forbes: http://www.forbes.com/sites/

zackomalleygreenburg/2014/04/18/jay-zs-net-
worth-520-million-in-2014/

http://www.nasdaq.com. (2015, 02 17). Retrieved 02 17, 2015,
from Nasdaq: http://www.nasdaq.com/symbol/
sbux/revenue-eps

Humes, M. (2013). Success is what you make it. In M. Humes,
Dominate your Life (p. 276). Georgia: Heaven on
Earth, Inc.

Humes, M. (2014). Retrieved 03 07, 2015, from RBR PR &
Advertising Agency: http://www.rbragency.com

http://www.fdic.gov/deposit/deposits/

http://nielson.com/us/aboutus , 85 Broad Street, New York,
NY 10004,+1 800-864-1224

GLOSSARY

Bling Posting

Posting with no agenda

Brand

What identifies you from the rest in your marketplace

Buyer's Market Supply

Outweighs demand

Celebrity

A brand that owns the spotlight

Consumers

A person who purchases your brands products or services

Diamond

A brand that has made it pass all the pressure & the process to shine bright

Entrepreneurial spirit

A soul that refuses to quit pushing forward as a boss, brand, in business, and in many endeavors,

regardless of what comes their way they
continue to build their own wealth

FDIC

Federal Deposit Insurance Corporation, an agency
created by US Congress, 877-275-3342

Howard Schultz

Owner of Starbucks

Illuminate

To provide light to, to lighten up, or to shine bright

IMC -Integrated Marketing Communications

Ways to gather consumer intelligence

Know

to perceive directly: have direct cognition of, to have
understanding of <importance of *knowing*
oneself> : to recognize the nature of

Kundalini

Energy that is located in the lower spine area, when
activated it awakens energy that can rise to
the brain to enlighten you. It can be activated
through yoga or meditational practices

4 P's of Marketing

Price, product, promotion, and placement

Mark Zuckenburg

CEO of Facebook

Mogul

An individual with kick ass ability as a boss that has
            built an empire

Moi

French for me

Powerhouse

A brand with a great authority, power, influence, and that
            has high levels of energy

PR

Public relation, a form of marketing

#PRGoddess

One with an impeccable ability to shine as the
            illuminating Goddess she is, to enforce the
            law, to brand as a boss, mogul, and carry the
            capabilities of a warrior and a beast, while
            remaining in her beautiful essence.

Publicity

Attention and exposure that is promoted and advertised
exclusively for your brand by media

Seller's Market Demand

Outweighs supply

Seth Godin

Author of Permission Marketing, Marketer

Smart Goals

Specific, Measurable, Action, Realistic, Timed

STP

Segmenting, Targeting, and Positioning

Uber

A private car that operates to pick you up with your own
personal driver